SACRED KNOWLEDGE OF UPNISHADS

ANANT KESHAV RATHOD

TANEESHA PUBLISHERS

Title   : Sacred Knowledge of Upnishads

Author   : Anant Keshav Rathod

Edition   : First (August, 2024)

ISBN   : 9788197599620

Published by

TANEESHA PUBLISHERS | A Venture by -
PRACHI DIGITAL PUBLICATION

Regd. Add.: 254, Khuriyakhatta No. 10, Bindukhatta,
Lalkuan, Nainital - 262402, Uttarakhand, India
Website : www.taneeshapublishers.in
E-mail : taneeshapublishers@gmail.com
Phone : +91 845481 2712, +91 976041 7980

Printed by :
Manipal Technologies Limited, Bengaluru - 560001, Karnataka

This book is dedicated to my father and
mother, whose hard work and sacrifice have
shaped my life.

Their unwavering support and love mean
everything to me.

INDEX

Author's Note

Welcome to "Sacred Knowledge of the Upanishads," a journey into the profound depths of ancient Indian wisdom. This book is an invitation to immerse yourself in the timeless teachings of the Upanishads, the philosophical and spiritual heart of Hinduism.

The Upanishads are revered as the culmination of the Vedic scriptures, offering insights that have shaped the spiritual landscape of India for millennia. From the secluded hermitages of ancient sages to the vibrant discourse of contemporary scholars, the Upanishads continue to illuminate the path of seekers with their profound and transformative wisdom.

Writing this book has been a deeply enriching experience. My goal has been to simplify and present the core teachings of the Upanishads in a way that is both accessible and applicable to modern life. In a world often dominated by the fleeting concerns of the material realm, the Upanishads offer a sanctuary of enduring truths and spiritual clarity.

Throughout this book, you will encounter the timeless principles of Atman (the self), Brahman (the ultimate reality), and the intricate interplay between the two. You will explore the concepts of Satyam (truth), Jnanam (knowledge), and Anantam (infinity), and discover how these teachings can guide you towards a life of deeper meaning and fulfillment. I am immensely grateful to the sages and scholars who have preserved and shared these sacred texts. Their dedication and insight have been a source of inspiration and guidance for countless generations.

First and foremost, I owe an immense debt of gratitude to Professor Dr. Avadhesh Pratap Singh and Professor Dr. Monica Kunwar Rathore. Their profound influence and mentorship have been pivotal in shaping my knowledge and understanding, particularly in the realms of philosophy and Sanskrit studies. Their guidance has not only deepened my academic insights but has also fostered a nuanced appreciation for the interconnectedness of philosophical thought and linguistic tradition. I am deeply grateful for their continuous support, encouragement, and unwavering belief in my academic journey.

I also extend my heartfelt gratitude to you, the reader, for embarking on this journey with an open heart and mind.

May "Sacred Knowledge of the Upanishads" serve as a beacon of wisdom and inspiration on your spiritual path. As you delve into these teachings, may you find not only knowledge but also a profound connection to the essence of your being and the infinite reality that surrounds us.

With deepest gratitude,
Anant Keshav Rathod

ईशावास्यमिदं सर्वं यत्किञ्च जगत्यां जगत् ।
तेन त्यक्तेन भुञ्जीथा मा गृधः कस्य स्विद्धनम् ॥ १ ॥

- ईशावास्योपनिषद्

All this is for habitation by the Lord, whatsoever is individual universe of movement in the universal motion. By that renounced thou shouldst enjoy; lust not after any man's possession.

The Upanishads

The Upanishads are ancient Indian texts that form the philosophical and spiritual foundation of Hinduism. They are considered the end or culmination of the Vedic scriptures, often referred to as Vedanta, meaning "the end of the Vedas." The term "Upanishad" is derived from the Sanskrit words "upa" (near), "ni" (down), and "shad" (to sit), signifying the tradition of disciples sitting close to their guru to receive esoteric wisdom.

These texts delve into profound spiritual concepts, exploring the nature of reality, the self (Atman), and the ultimate reality (Brahman). The Upanishads seek to answer fundamental questions about existence, consciousness, and the ultimate purpose of life. They shift focus from the ritualistic and sacrificial aspects of the earlier Vedas to a more philosophical and introspective inquiry.

Historical Context

The Upanishads were composed over several centuries, with scholars estimating their creation from around 800 BCE to 500 BCE, and some later texts emerging in subsequent centuries. They mark a significant evolution in Vedic thought, transitioning from the external rituals and hymns of the early Vedic period to the internal quest for knowledge and enlightenment.

This period in Indian history saw the rise of small kingdoms and republics in the Ganges Plain, a region marked by intellectual and spiritual ferment. The teachings of the Upanishads reflect a time of questioning and seeking deeper understanding, as sages and seers moved away from the purely ritualistic practices of the Vedas towards a philosophical inquiry into the nature of the universe and the self.

Structure and Classification of the Upanishads

The Upanishads are part of the later Vedic literature and are classified into different groups based on their association with the four Vedas: the Rigveda, Yajurveda, Samaveda, and Atharvaveda. They are primarily prose texts, although some contain poetic passages. The Upanishads are diverse in form, length, and content, but they all share a common goal of exploring the ultimate truth.

The principal Upanishads, often considered the most important and influential, include:

Isha Upanishad

The Isha Upanishad is one of the shortest and most profound texts, consisting of just 18 verses. It emphasizes the unity of the individual soul (Atman) and the supreme soul (Brahman), advocating a balanced life of action and renunciation. The text begins with the assertion that the entire universe is pervaded by the divine essence, urging individuals to enjoy the world without attachment. It explores the relationship between knowledge and ignorance, action and renunciation, and the inner and outer worlds.

Kena Upanishad

The Kena Upanishad explores the nature of the ultimate reality and the limitations of human senses and intellect in comprehending it. It is presented as a dialogue between a student and a teacher, where the student inquires about the force behind perception and consciousness. The teacher explains that it is Brahman, the ultimate reality, which is beyond the grasp of the senses and mind. The text highlights the paradoxical nature of Brahman, which is known through direct experience rather than intellectual understanding.

Katha Upanishad

The Katha Upanishad is a dialogue between the young seeker Nachiketa and Yama, the god of death. It addresses the nature of the self, the cycle of birth and death, and the path to immortality through self-knowledge and detachment. Nachiketa's quest begins with questions about the afterlife and the nature of the self. Yama teaches him about the eternal and indestructible nature of Atman, which is beyond birth and death. The text emphasizes the importance of discerning the transient from the eternal and choosing the path of knowledge and wisdom.

Prashna Upanishad

The Prashna Upanishad consists of six questions posed by six seekers to the sage Pippalada. It delves into topics such as the origin of the universe, the nature of life forces (Prana), and the relationship between the individual and the cosmic self. Each question addresses a fundamental aspect of existence, and Pippalada's answers provide insights into the interconnectedness of the physical and spiritual realms. The text emphasizes the importance of understanding Prana as the vital force that sustains life and connects the individual to the cosmos.

Mundaka Upanishad

The Mundaka Upanishad distinguishes between higher knowledge (Para Vidya) and lower knowledge (Apara Vidya). It emphasizes the importance of realizing Brahman, the ultimate reality, as the path to liberation. The text uses the metaphor of two birds sitting on the same tree to illustrate the relationship between the individual self and the higher self. One bird eats the fruit of the tree, representing the experiences of the material world, while the other bird, the witness, remains detached. The Upanishad teaches that true knowledge comes from recognizing the unity of the self with Brahman.

Mandukya Upanishad

The Mandukya Upanishad is the shortest of the principal Upanishads, consisting of just 12 verses. It explores the nature of consciousness through the analysis of the syllable "Om," describing the states of waking, dreaming, deep sleep, and the transcendental state of Turiya. The text explains that "Om" represents the totality of existence and consciousness, with each state corresponding to a part of the syllable. Turiya, the fourth state, is beyond the other three and represents pure consciousness and the ultimate reality.

Taittiriya Upanishad

The Taittiriya Upanishad consists of three sections, dealing with the nature of the self, the importance of truth and ethical conduct, and the unity of all existence. It presents the concept of the five sheaths (Koshas) that cover the true self: the physical body, the vital force, the mind, the intellect, and the blissful sheath. The Upanishad teaches that the self is beyond these sheaths and is identical to

Brahman. It emphasizes the practice of truth, righteousness, and self-discipline as means to realize the self.

Aitareya Upanishad

The Aitareya Upanishad discusses the creation of the universe and the nature of the self. It describes how the supreme reality manifests as the individual soul and the world, emphasizing the realization of this unity. The text explains that Brahman created the world through a process of self-manifestation and that the individual self is a reflection of the cosmic self. The Upanishad teaches that by realizing the true nature of the self, one can transcend the limitations of the material world and attain liberation.

Chandogya Upanishad

The Chandogya Upanishad is one of the largest Upanishads, containing various dialogues and stories that illustrate the nature of reality and the self. It includes the famous Mahavakya (great saying) "Tat Tvam Asi" (That Thou Art), affirming the identity of the individual soul with Brahman. The text explores the interconnectedness of the universe, the power of sound and speech, and the importance of meditation and ethical conduct. It teaches that by understanding the unity of all existence, one can achieve self-realization and liberation.

Brihadaranyaka Upanishad

The Brihadaranyaka Upanishad is one of the most comprehensive and profound texts, exploring the nature of reality, the self, and the universe through dialogues and philosophical discourses. It includes discussions on the nature of consciousness, the ultimate goal of liberation, and the identity of the individual self with Brahman. The text emphasizes the importance of knowledge, meditation, and ethical conduct as means to attain self-realization and liberation. It teaches that the true self is beyond the physical and mental limitations and is identical to the ultimate reality.

Central Themes and Concepts

The Upanishads introduce several key concepts that have become central to Indian philosophy. These include:

1. **Brahman**: The ultimate, unchanging reality, which is infinite, eternal, and beyond human comprehension. Brahman is described as the source and essence of everything in the universe. It is the underlying reality that transcends all forms and phenomena.

- **Saguna Brahman**: Brahman with attributes, perceived through various forms and deities.
- **Nirguna Brahman**: Brahman without attributes, the formless, infinite, and unmanifested reality.

2. **Atman**: The individual self or soul, which is considered to be identical with Brahman. The realization of this unity is the ultimate goal of spiritual practice. Atman is the innermost essence of an individual, beyond the physical body and mind.

3. **Maya**: The cosmic illusion or appearance that veils the true nature of reality. Maya is the power that creates the phenomenal world, making it appear as real and diverse, although it is ultimately illusory. Understanding and transcending Maya is crucial for spiritual liberation.

4. **Karma**: The law of cause and effect, where every action has

consequences that shape one's future experiences. Karma operates on the principle of moral causation, where good actions lead to positive outcomes and bad actions lead to negative outcomes. It influences the cycle of birth, death, and rebirth (samsara).

5. **Samsara**: The cycle of birth, death, and rebirth, driven by karma and characterized by suffering and impermanence. Samsara represents the endless cycle of existence, where beings undergo repeated births and deaths due to their actions. The ultimate aim is to break free from this cycle.

6. **Moksha**: Liberation from the cycle of samsara, achieved through the realization of the self's unity with Brahman. Moksha is the state of eternal bliss, peace, and freedom, where the individual soul merges with the ultimate reality and transcends all limitations.

7. **Jnana**: Knowledge or wisdom, particularly the knowledge of the self and the ultimate reality. Jnana is not merely intellectual understanding but direct experiential realization, which leads to liberation.

8. **Shruti**: The revealed texts, considered to be of divine origin and passed down through an unbroken tradition. The Upanishads are part of the shruti literature, regarded as authoritative and eternal truths revealed to the ancient sages.

The Path to Knowledge

The Upanishads emphasize the importance of self-inquiry and meditation as the means to attain spiritual knowledge. The path to understanding the true nature of the self and the universe involves several stages:

1. **Shravana (Listening)**: Hearing the teachings of the Upanishads from a qualified teacher (guru). The first step in acquiring knowledge is to listen attentively to the scriptures and the words of wisdom imparted by the guru. This requires a receptive mind and an open heart.

2. **Manana (Reflection)**: Reflecting deeply on these teachings to assimilate their meaning. After listening, one must engage in deep contemplation and rational analysis of the teachings. This process involves questioning, reasoning, and resolving doubts to gain a clear understanding.

3. **Nididhyasana (Meditation)**: Meditating on the truths revealed in the Upanishads to realize them directly. The final step is to internalize the teachings through meditation and constant practice. This involves focusing the mind, withdrawing from external distractions, and experiencing the truths at a deeper, intuitive level.

4. **Vairagya (Dispassion)**: Developing detachment from the material world and its transient pleasures. Dispassion is essential for spiritual progress, as it helps to overcome

attachments and desires that bind one to the cycle of samsara. It cultivates a sense of inner renunciation and a focus on the higher reality.

5. **Sadhana (Spiritual Practice)**: Engaging in disciplined and sustained spiritual practices. Sadhana includes practices such as meditation, chanting, selfless service, and ethical living. It helps purify the mind, strengthen the will, and deepen the understanding of the Upanishadic teachings.

Influence on Indian Philosophy and Beyond

The philosophical ideas of the Upanishads have had a profound influence on various schools of Indian philosophy. Some of the major schools that have drawn heavily from Upanishadic teachings include:

1. **Advaita Vedanta**: A non-dualistic school founded by Adi Shankaracharya, which asserts the essential oneness of the individual soul (Atman) and the ultimate reality (Brahman). According to Advaita, the perception of duality is an illusion created by ignorance (avidya). Realizing the unity of Atman and Brahman leads to liberation.

2. **Vishishtadvaita Vedanta**: A qualified non-dualistic school founded by Ramanuja, which acknowledges the oneness of Brahman but sees the individual souls and the universe as real and distinct parts of Brahman. Vishishtadvaita emphasizes the concept of qualified monism, where the soul is a part of Brahman but retains its individuality.

3. **Dvaita Vedanta**: A dualistic school founded by Madhvacharya, which maintains a clear distinction between the individual soul (jiva) and the supreme reality (Brahman). According to Dvaita, the soul and Brahman are eternally separate, and liberation involves realizing the soul's dependence on Brahman.

4. **Yoga**: The philosophy and practice of Yoga, as outlined in the Yoga Sutras of Patanjali, also draw upon Upanishadic concepts. Yoga emphasizes the control of the mind and senses, the cultivation of inner awareness, and the attainment of union with the ultimate reality.

5. **Samkhya**: An ancient dualistic school that posits two fundamental principles: Purusha (consciousness) and Prakriti (matter). While distinct from the monistic approach of the Upanishads, Samkhya's exploration of the nature of consciousness and its separation from material existence resonates with Upanishadic themes.

6. **Nyaya and Vaisheshika**: Schools of logic and metaphysics that, while focusing on systematic inquiry and categorization, also incorporate Upanishadic insights into the nature of knowledge, perception, and the self.

The Upanishads have also inspired Western philosophers and writers. German philosopher Arthur Schopenhauer praised the Upanishads as the highest human wisdom. Translations and interpretations by scholars such as Max Müller, Ralph Waldo Emerson, Aldous Huxley, and T.S. Eliot have introduced Upanishadic teachings to a global audience, influencing modern spiritual and philosophical thought.

The Relevance of the Upanishads Today

In today's fast-paced and often chaotic world, the teachings of the Upanishads offer timeless wisdom that can help individuals find inner peace and purpose. The emphasis on self-knowledge, mindfulness, and the interconnectedness of all life resonates with contemporary spiritual seekers and those looking to lead a more meaningful existence.

1. **Mindfulness and Meditation**: The practice of mindfulness and meditation, which is central to the Upanishadic tradition, has gained widespread popularity in modern times. These practices help reduce stress, enhance mental clarity, and foster a sense of inner calm and well-being.

2. **Self-Inquiry and Personal Growth**: The Upanishads encourage individuals to engage in self-inquiry and introspection, leading to personal growth and self-realization. This inward journey helps individuals understand their true nature and purpose, beyond external identities and roles.

3. **Ethical Living and Compassion**: The Upanishadic teachings emphasize the importance of ethical living, compassion, and non-violence (ahimsa). These values are essential for creating

harmonious relationships and fostering a sense of interconnectedness and empathy in society.

4. **Environmental Awareness**: The recognition of the interconnectedness of all life forms in the Upanishads aligns with modern environmental consciousness. The understanding that all beings are part of the same universal essence can inspire a deeper respect for nature and a commitment to environmental sustainability.

5. **Spiritual Fulfillment**: In a world driven by material pursuits and external achievements, the Upanishads remind us of the importance of spiritual fulfillment. They offer insights into finding lasting happiness and contentment through inner realization and connection with the ultimate reality.

The Upanishads represent a monumental achievement in human thought, offering profound insights into the nature of reality and the self. Their teachings have endured for thousands of years, guiding countless individuals on their spiritual journeys. As we delve into the teachings of the Upanishads, we embark on a path of self-discovery and spiritual awakening that has the potential to transform our lives and bring us closer to the ultimate truth.

In the following chapters, we will explore the key teachings of the major Upanishads, delving deeper into their philosophy and understanding how their wisdom can be applied to our modern lives. Through this exploration, may we find the inspiration and guidance to live with greater clarity, compassion, and fulfillment.

Who Is Ishawara ?

The Isha Upanishad, also known as the Isavasya Upanishad, is one of the shortest yet most profound Hindu scriptures. It is part of the Yajur Veda, specifically the Shukla Yajur Veda, and is considered a major Upanishad. The name "Isha" comes from the Sanskrit root "Ish," which means "to rule" or "to command." In this context, it refers to the Supreme Being or Lord who is present everywhere in the universe.

This Upanishad is unique because it is very concise, with just 18 verses. Despite its brevity, it offers a complete and holistic philosophy of life. It talks about the presence of the divine in everything and emphasizes living a balanced life that harmonizes material and spiritual pursuits.

To fully understand the teachings of the Isha Upanishad, it's helpful to know its historical and philosophical background. The Upanishads, often called Vedanta (meaning "the end of the Vedas"), represent the ultimate wisdom of the Vedic tradition. They contain the philosophical and mystical thoughts of ancient Indian sages, going beyond the ritualistic aspects of the Vedas to explore the nature of reality, the self, and the ultimate truth.

The Isha Upanishad stands out due to its poetic and aphoristic style, its emphasis on the unity of all existence, and its call for a life of detachment and duty. It addresses deep metaphysical questions while offering practical advice for living in the world without being overly attached to it.

Structure and Content of the Isha Upanishad

The 18 verses of the Isha Upanishad can be grouped into three broad themes: the omnipresence of the divine, the path of action, and the distinction between knowledge and ignorance.

Verses 1-2: The Omnipresence of the Divine

The Upanishad begins with the famous declaration:

"ॐ Isha vasyam idam sarvam yat kinca jagatyam jagat."

This means, "All this—whatever exists in this changing universe—should be covered by the Lord." This opening statement sets the tone for the entire Upanishad, asserting that the divine is present in every aspect of the universe. It emphasizes that God is not distant or separate from creation but is intimately present in every part of it.

The second verse continues this theme, advising that one should enjoy the wealth of the world without attachment:

"Ten tyaktena bhunjitha, ma gridhah kasya svid dhanam."

This translates to "By the renunciation of worldly desires, enjoy the world. Do not covet anyone's wealth." Here, the Upanishad introduces the concept of renunciation—not as an abandonment of life but as a means of enjoying life without becoming attached to it. It advocates for a balanced approach where one can live fully and engage with the world while maintaining a sense of detachment and humility.

Verses 3-8: The Path of Action and Inaction

Verses 3 to 8 explore the interplay between action (karma) and renunciation (sannyasa). They discuss the idea that while physical actions are necessary, they should be performed without attachment to the results. This theme aligns closely with the teachings of the Bhagavad Gita, another key text in Hindu philosophy, which emphasizes performing one's duty (dharma) without attachment to the fruits of the actions (karma-phala).

Verse 3 warns of the consequences of a life driven by ignorance and attachment:

"Asurya nama te loka andhena tamasavrtah."

This means, "The worlds of the demons are enshrouded in blinding darkness." It cautions against living a life focused solely on material pursuits and sensory pleasures, which leads to spiritual blindness and suffering.

Verses 4 and 5 present a paradox, describing the nature of the Atman (the self):

"Tad ejati tan naijati, tad dure tad v antike."

"It moves, it moves not, it is far, it is near."

These verses highlight the mysterious and paradoxical nature of the self, which transcends ordinary dualistic distinctions. The self is beyond the grasp of the senses and the mind, yet it is ever-present and intimately close to us.

Verses 6 and 7 further elaborate on the nature of the self, emphasizing its omnipresence and the unity of all beings. The realization of this unity leads to a life of compassion and selflessness:

"Yasmin sarvani bhutani atmaivabhud vijanatah, tatra ko mohah kah shokah ekatvam anupasyatah."

"One who sees all beings in the self and the self in all beings, no longer suffers from delusion and sorrow." This profound realization of the interconnectedness of all life is a cornerstone of the Isha Upanishad's teachings.

Verse 8 concludes this section with a meditation on the nature of the self as pure consciousness and bliss

"Sa paryagac chukram akayam avranam."

"The self is pure, unembodied, untouched by sin." This verse reinforces the idea that the true self is beyond the physical body and the limitations of worldly existence.

Verses 9-14: Knowledge and Ignorance

Verses 9 to 14 explore the distinction between vidya (knowledge) and avidya (ignorance). These verses emphasize that true knowledge transcends intellectual understanding and involves a direct realization of the self.

Verse 9 warns against the dangers of ignorance:

"Andham tamah pravisanti ye avidyam upasate."

"Those who worship ignorance enter into darkness." This verse cautions against the pursuit of purely materialistic goals and the neglect of spiritual wisdom.

Verses 10 and 11 present a nuanced view, suggesting that both knowledge and ignorance have their roles:

"Vidyam cavidyam ca yas tad vedobhayam saha."

"One who knows both knowledge and ignorance together, crosses death through ignorance and attains immortality through knowledge." This paradoxical statement highlights the importance of balancing worldly knowledge with spiritual insight.

Verses 12 to 14 further explore this theme, contrasting the paths of knowledge and ignorance and emphasizing the ultimate goal of self-realization.

Verses 15-18: Prayer for Enlightenment

The final verses of the Isha Upanishad are prayers for enlightenment and liberation. They express a deep yearning for the direct experience of the divine and the transcendence of the limitations of the physical body.

Verse 15 is a plea to the divine:

"Hiranyamayena patrena satyasya apihitam mukham."

"The face of truth is hidden by a golden vessel." This verse symbolizes the idea that the ultimate truth is obscured by the illusions of the material world and the limitations of human perception.

Verses 16 and 17 continue this prayer, asking for the divine light to reveal the true self and guide the seeker to liberation:

"Pusan ekarse yama surya prajapatya."

"O nourishing Sun, sole traveler of the heavens, controller of all, withdraw your rays and gather up your light; I would see through your grace that form of yours which is your fairest."

Verse 18 concludes the Upanishad with a final invocation for liberation:

"Agne naya supatha raye asman."

"O Fire, lead us by the good path to eternal joy, O God, who knowest all ways." This final verse encapsulates the aspirant's desire for divine guidance and the ultimate realization of the self.

Practical Implications of the Isha Upanishad

The teachings of the Isha Upanishad are not merely abstract philosophical concepts but practical guidelines for living a balanced and fulfilling life. Here are some key practical implications of its teachings:

1. Living a Balanced Life

The Isha Upanishad advocates for a life that balances material and spiritual pursuits. It teaches that one can enjoy the world and its pleasures without becoming attached to them. This balanced approach allows individuals to fulfill their worldly responsibilities while maintaining a sense of detachment and inner peace.

2. Performing Duties Without Attachment

The Upanishad emphasizes the importance of performing one's duties without attachment to the results. This principle, known as nishkama karma, encourages individuals to focus on their actions and responsibilities without being overly concerned with the outcomes. This attitude leads to a more peaceful and contented life.

3. Recognizing the Unity of All Beings

The realization that the same divine essence pervades all beings leads to a life of compassion, selflessness, and respect for all forms of life. This understanding fosters a sense of unity and interconnectedness, reducing conflicts and promoting harmony in society.

4. Embracing Both Knowledge and Ignorance

The Isha Upanishad's nuanced view of knowledge and ignorance encourages individuals to seek a balance between intellectual understanding and spiritual wisdom. It teaches that true knowledge involves a direct realization of the self, which transcends mere intellectual understanding.

5. Seeking Enlightenment

The prayers for enlightenment in the final verses of the Upanishad reflect the aspirant's deep yearning for direct experience of the divine. This aspiration encourages individuals to pursue spiritual practices that lead to self-realization and liberation.

The Isha Upanishad, though brief, encapsulates the essence of the Upanishadic wisdom. Its teachings emphasize the omnipresence of the divine, the importance of living a balanced life, the need for detachment and duty, the recognition of the unity of all beings, and the pursuit of true knowledge and enlightenment. By integrating these teachings into daily life, individuals can attain inner peace, harmony, and ultimately, liberation.

The Isha Upanishad remains a timeless guide, offering profound insights and practical wisdom that continue to inspire and guide seekers of truth across the world. Its message of unity, detachment, and spiritual aspiration resonates deeply, reminding us of the eternal truths that lie at the heart of the human experience

Who Is Brahma ?

The Kena Upanishad, also known as the Talavakara Upanishad, is one of the primary Upanishads embedded in the Samaveda. Listed as the second Upanishad in the Muktikā canon of 108 Upanishads, this text is crucial in the philosophical and spiritual landscape of Hinduism. Composed around the middle of the 1st millennium BCE, the Kena Upanishad is distinguished by its unique structure and profound teachings on the nature of Brahman, the ultimate reality, and knowledge.

The Kena Upanishad's structure includes a combination of verses and prose, reflecting the transition from ancient prose Upanishads to the more poetic Upanishads. The first 13 verses are composed as a metric poem, followed by 15 prose paragraphs and a 6-paragraph epilogue. This composition bridges the gap between different eras of Upanishadic literature.

The Kena Upanishad is divided into four sections, called Khandas:

First Khanda: Nature of Knowledge

The Upanishad begins with a series of profound questions exploring the origins and essence of man, the nature of knowledge, and the relationship between sensory perception and the divine. The opening verse poses these questions:

"Sent by whom does the mind fly out?

Who harnesses the breath?

Who sends out the speech we speak?

Who harnesses the eyes and ears?"

These questions set the stage for a deep inquiry into the nature of reality and consciousness. The Upanishad then makes a critical distinction between two types of knowledge: empirical knowledge and conceptual knowledge.

Empirical Knowledge: This type of knowledge can be taught, described, and discussed. It is based on sensory perception and intellectual analysis.

Conceptual Knowledge: This type of knowledge is abstract and realized through direct experience. It is the understanding of pure, axiomatic concepts that transcend empirical observation.

The Kena Upanishad asserts that the highest reality is Brahman, which cannot be comprehended through empirical means. Brahman is beyond sensory perception and intellectual comprehension. It is the eternal, all-present reality that "hears" through the ears, "sees" through the eyes, "beholds" through speech, "smells" through the breath, and "comprehends" through the mind.

In verse 4, the Upanishad emphasizes that Brahman cannot be worshipped because it has no attributes and is unthinkable. It is not an object of worship but the essence of all existence. This teaching underscores the difference between the empirical worship of deities and the realization of the formless, attribute-less Brahman.

Second Khanda: Self-Awakening and Inner Strength

The second Khanda begins with prose paragraph 9, which introduces a theistic theme, suggesting that the worship of Brahman as described in the first Khanda is a deception because it is a phenomenal form of Brahman, one among many gods. This paragraph is considered out of place by scholars, indicating a possible later insertion or corruption of the original text.

The text then returns to poetry, continuing the exploration of what it means to know Brahman. Verses 10 to 13 describe the state of self-realization (moksha). These verses assert that self-awakening brings inner strength and the realization of the Spiritual Oneness in all beings, leading to immortality. "He who has found it here below, possesses the truth. For him who has not found it here, it is great destruction. In every being, the wise being perceives it, and departing out of this world, becomes immortal."

These verses highlight that those who realize Brahman while living attain true knowledge and immortality. This state of self-awareness is described as the "Spiritual Man," characterized by inner strength and the perception of the divine essence in all beings.

Third and Fourth Khandas: Allegory of the Three Gods and the Epilogue

The third section of the Kena Upanishad shifts to a prose format, presenting a fable that serves as an allegory. This story illustrates the limitations of empirical knowledge and the nature of Brahman.

The Allegory of the Three Gods

The fable begins with a war between the gods (Devas) and demons (Asuras). The gods win the battle, but they attribute the victory to themselves, failing to recognize Brahman's role. Brahman then reveals itself before the gods, who do not recognize it. The gods send Agni (the god of fire) to discover the identity of this wonderful being. Agni approaches Brahman, who asks, "Who are you?" Agni replies, "I am Agni, the knower of beings." Brahman then asks, "What is the source of your power?" Agni responds, "I can burn whatever is on earth." Brahman challenges Agni to burn a piece of grass, but Agni fails and returns to the gods, admitting his inability to discover the being's identity.

Next, the gods send Vayu (the god of air) to investigate. Vayu encounters Brahman, who asks the same questions. Vayu claims his power is to carry or pull whatever is on earth. Brahman challenges him to lift the piece of grass, but Vayu also fails and returns to the gods. Finally, the gods send Indra (the god of lightning and might) to explore the wonderful being. Indra finds a beautiful woman, Uma, who reveals that the being is Brahman, the true victor of the battle. Indra realizes the truth and gains the highest knowledge.

This allegory is rich in symbolism. Agni represents the natural self and vital fire in all beings, Vayu symbolizes the mental self and thoughts, and Indra embodies the causal conscious self and the light of truth. The goddess Uma signifies wisdom and the revelation of spiritual knowledge.

The story teaches that empirical actions and sensory perceptions cannot lead to the true knowledge of Brahman. The victory of good over evil is not of the manifested self but of the eternal Atman-Brahman. The gods' realization of Brahman symbolizes the awakening of inner knowledge and the understanding of the ultimate reality.

Epilogue

The epilogue of the Kena Upanishad, contained in the last six paragraphs, emphasizes the timelessness and awareness of Brahman. It compares the realization of Brahman to moments of wondrous exclamation, such as witnessing a lightning flash or recalling a profound memory. The text asserts that the goal of spiritual knowledge and self-awareness is characterized by an intense longing in all creatures. The Upanishad concludes by asserting that ethical life is the foundation of self-knowledge and understanding of Atman-Brahman. It emphasizes the importance of self-discipline (tapas), ethical behavior (dama), and truthful living:

"Tapas, Damah, Work - these are the foundations, the Vedas are the limbs of the same, the Truth is its fulcrum."

Practical Implications

The teachings of the Kena Upanishad offer practical guidance for living a balanced and fulfilling life:

1. **Balancing Material and Spiritual Pursuits**: The Upanishad teaches the importance of enjoying the world without attachment, harmonizing material and spiritual pursuits. It encourages individuals to seek a balance between worldly

responsibilities and spiritual growth.

2. **Performing Duties Without Attachment**: The text emphasizes the value of performing actions and fulfilling responsibilities without attachment to outcomes. This approach leads to inner peace and spiritual progress.

3. **Recognizing the Unity of All Beings**: The realization of the divine essence in all beings fosters compassion, selflessness, and harmony. Understanding that Brahman is present in every being promotes a sense of unity and interconnectedness.

4. **Balancing Knowledge**: The Kena Upanishad distinguishes between empirical and conceptual knowledge. It encourages the pursuit of both, recognizing the limitations of intellectual understanding and the importance of spiritual wisdom.

5. **Aspiring for Enlightenment**: The Upanishad advocates for spiritual practices that lead to self-realization and liberation. It emphasizes the importance of ethical living, self-discipline, and the pursuit of truth.

The Kena Upanishad, though brief, offers profound philosophical insights and practical wisdom. Its teachings on the nature of Brahman, the importance of self-realization, and the value of ethical living remain timeless. By exploring the essence of knowledge and the eternal reality, the Kena Upanishad guides seekers of truth towards inner peace and ultimate liberation.

Through its poetic verses, prose allegories, and profound philosophical assertions, the Kena Upanishad continues to inspire and enlighten those on the path of spiritual discovery.

What Happens After Death?

The **Katha Upanishad** is a very old Hindu text that is one of the key Upanishads, which are important spiritual writings in Hinduism. It is part of the last eight sections of the Kaṭha school of the Krishna Yajurveda. Sometimes it is also called the **Kāṭhaka Upanishad** and is listed as number 3 in the Muktika collection of 108 Upanishads.

In ancient times, there was a wise and devout Brahmin named Vajasrava. Vajasrava was known for his strict adherence to Vedic rituals and spiritual practices. He aspired to attain the highest realms of the afterlife and believed that performing a grand Yajna (sacrifice) would help him achieve this. In this sacred ritual, he gave away all his possessions as gifts to priests and attendees, symbolizing his detachment from worldly attachments.

However, Vajasrava's intentions were not entirely pure. Among the possessions he gave away were old and infirm cows, which were no longer useful for agricultural work or providing milk. This act, although seemingly generous, was inappropriate for such a sacred ritual. It was in this context that Vajasrava's young son, Nachiketa, began to question the true nature of sacrifice, duty, and righteousness.

Nachiketa's Concern and Inquiry

Nachiketa, a young boy endowed with wisdom and a keen sense of righteousness, watched his father's actions closely. He saw the old and weak cows being given away and felt uneasy. He pondered the true nature of sacrifice and whether his father's offerings would yield the desired spiritual benefits. Nachiketa's contemplative nature led him to ask his father a profound question: "Father, to whom will you give me?"

Nachiketa asked this question repeatedly, each time with increasing urgency. His father, absorbed in the ritual and perhaps annoyed by his son's persistence, finally responded in a moment of frustration, saying, "I give you to Death (Yama)!" These words, spoken in anger, were taken seriously by Nachiketa. He believed in the sanctity of his father's word and decided to honor it by seeking out Yama, the god of death. Determined to fulfill his father's hasty declaration, Nachiketa embarked on a journey to the abode of Yama. The path to the realm of the god of death was fraught with challenges, symbolizing the arduous journey of a seeker in pursuit of spiritual knowledge. Nachiketa's unwavering resolve and commitment to truth guided him through this difficult journey.

Upon reaching Yama's abode, Nachiketa found that Yama was not present. Demonstrating immense patience and fortitude, he waited for three days and nights without food or water. This period of waiting symbolized the tests and trials that a seeker must endure on the path to enlightenment. Nachiketa's endurance and commitment did not go unnoticed. When Yama returned, he was deeply moved by the young boy's determination and patience.

Yama's Offer of Three Boons

As a gesture of atonement for making Nachiketa wait, Yama offered him three boons. This offer was not just a recompense but also an opportunity for Nachiketa to seek profound knowledge and understanding.

First Boon: Reconciliation with His Father

For his first boon, Nachiketa asked that his father's anger be pacified and that he be welcomed home with love and without any ill will. This request reflected Nachiketa's deep sense of duty and filial piety. He wanted to ensure that his father would not suffer the consequences of his rash words and that their relationship would remain harmonious. Yama granted this boon readily, assuring Nachiketa that his father's anger would subside and that he would be welcomed back with open arms. This boon highlighted the importance of maintaining harmonious relationships and the power of forgiveness and understanding.

Second Boon: Knowledge of the Sacred Fire Ritual

For his second boon, Nachiketa sought knowledge of the sacred fire ritual (Nachiketa Agni) that leads to heaven, a realm free from fear, old age, and death. This request demonstrated Nachiketa's intellectual curiosity and his desire to understand the deeper aspects of Vedic rituals. Yama, pleased with this noble request, taught Nachiketa the intricacies of the fire sacrifice. He explained the precise methods and recitations required to perform the ritual correctly. Nachiketa, with his sharp intellect, absorbed the teachings and repeated them flawlessly. This act of learning and mastery earned Yama's admiration and further established Nachiketa's sincerity as a seeker of truth.

The knowledge of the sacred fire ritual symbolized the pursuit of righteous actions (karma) and the benefits they confer both in the material and spiritual realms. It also underscored the importance of discipline, precision, and dedication in spiritual practice.

Third Boon: The Mystery of What Lies Beyond Death

For his final boon, Nachiketa asked the profound question that had perplexed humanity for ages: "What happens after death? Does the soul exist after death, or does it perish?" This question went to the heart of existential inquiry and sought to unravel the deepest mysteries of life and death.

Yama was taken aback by the profundity of Nachiketa's question. He acknowledged the complexity and depth of the inquiry and initially tried to dissuade Nachiketa from pursuing this line of questioning. Yama offered him various temptations: long life, wealth, and power—everything that an ordinary person might desire. But Nachiketa remained steadfast, showing his genuine thirst for true knowledge over transient pleasures.

Yama's Teachings: The Eternal Self

Impressed by Nachiketa's determination and maturity, Yama decided to impart the profound knowledge of the eternal self

(Atman). The teachings that followed formed the essence of the Katha Upanishad, exploring the nature of the self, the impermanence of material pleasures, and the path to spiritual liberation.

The Impermanence of Material Pleasures

Yama began by explaining that material pleasures are temporary and ultimately unsatisfying. They are distractions that can lead one away from the path of true understanding. Real happiness and fulfillment lie in realizing the nature of the self. Yama used the metaphor of a chariot to illustrate this point, where the body is the chariot, the self is the charioteer, and the senses are the horses. The wise person, who has control over the senses and the mind, reaches the ultimate destination of self-realization.

The Nature of the Self

Yama described the self as eternal, immortal, and indestructible. The self is beyond birth and death, untouched by physical and mental changes. It is like a spark of divinity within every being. Yama explained that the self is the ultimate reality, the source of all existence, and the foundation of consciousness. This teaching emphasized the indestructibility and immortality of the self, using metaphors to describe its attributes:

- **Immortality of the Soul**: The soul (Atman) is not subject to decay or destruction. Weapons cannot cut it, fire cannot burn it, water cannot wet it, and wind cannot dry it. The self is immutable, eternal, and transcends physical existence.

- **Realization of the Self**: True wisdom involves understanding and experiencing this immortal self. This realization brings liberation (moksha) from the cycle of birth and death (samsara).

- **The Path to Self-Realization**
- Yama explained the importance of self-discipline, ethical living, and spiritual practices. He highlighted that one must choose the path of wisdom (Shrayas) over the path of pleasure (Preyas). The path of wisdom leads to self-realization, while the path of pleasure keeps one entangled in the cycle of birth and death.

- **Meditation and Introspection**: Yama taught that through meditation and introspection, one can quiet the mind and perceive the true nature of the self. The self is realized not through intellectual reasoning but through direct experience.

- **Detachment and Discrimination**: Practicing detachment from material desires and discriminating between the real and the unreal are essential steps on the spiritual path. Understanding that the physical world is transient and that the self is eternal helps one prioritize spiritual growth over material accumulation.

The Wisdom of Nachiketa: Deepening the Inquiry

Nachiketa listened intently to Yama's teachings. His profound questions continued to explore the subtleties of existence, life, and death. Each question and answer revealed deeper layers of understanding, guiding him closer to the ultimate truth.

- **The Nature of True Knowledge**: Nachiketa asked about the nature of true knowledge and how one can distinguish between what is eternal and what is transient. Yama explained that true knowledge is the realization of the self, which is eternal and unchanging. All other knowledge pertains to the physical world, which is subject to change and decay.

- Yama emphasized that true knowledge comes from within and is realized through self-inquiry and meditation. It is not merely intellectual understanding but a direct experience of the self. This realization brings about a profound transformation in one's perception and understanding of reality.

- **The Role of the Guru (Teacher)**: Nachiketa inquired about the importance of having a guru or teacher on the spiritual path. Yama explained that a guru plays a crucial role in guiding the seeker towards self-realization. The guru, having attained self-knowledge, can illuminate the path for the disciple, helping to overcome obstacles and misconceptions.

- Yama highlighted that the relationship between the guru and the disciple is based on trust, respect, and dedication. The guru imparts wisdom through teachings, personal example, and direct transmission of spiritual energy. The disciple, in turn, must approach the guru with humility, sincerity, and an open heart.

- **The Power of Faith and Devotion**: Nachiketa asked about the role of faith and devotion in the pursuit of self-realization. Yama explained that faith (shraddha) and devotion (bhakti) are essential components of the spiritual path. Faith is the unwavering belief in the teachings of the scriptures and the words of the guru. It provides the foundation for spiritual practice and keeps the seeker motivated and focused.

- Devotion is the deep love and reverence for the divine. It opens the heart and connects the seeker to the source of all existence. Yama explained that through faith and devotion, one can cultivate inner purity, surrender the ego, and experience the divine presence within.

- **The Significance of Death and Rebirth**: Nachiketa's curiosity about the nature of death and rebirth led him to ask Yama about the significance of these phenomena. Yama explained that death is a natural transition from one state of existence to another. The physical body perishes, but the soul (Atman) continues its journey.

- Yama described the cycle of birth and death (samsara) as a process driven by karma (the law of cause and effect). The actions performed in one life determine the circumstances of future lives. Liberation (moksha) is attained when one realizes the true nature of the self and transcends the cycle of samsara.

- **The Inner Light and the Journey Within**: Yama spoke about the inner light, the divine spark within every being. He explained that this inner light is the source of all life and consciousness. It is the true self, the Atman, which is eternal and unchanging.

- Yama encouraged Nachiketa to embark on the journey within, to explore the depths of his own consciousness and discover the inner light. He explained that through meditation, self-inquiry, and devotion, one can transcend the limitations of the physical world and experience the infinite nature of the self.

Nachiketa's Enlightenment

Nachiketa listened intently to Yama's teachings. He grasped the profound truths and internalized them. Through his unwavering dedication and Yama's guidance, Nachiketa attained a deep understanding of the self and the nature of reality. He realized the immortal essence within him and the interconnectedness of all life.

With his newfound wisdom, Nachiketa returned home. His father, Vajasrava, welcomed him with open arms, and they both shared the knowledge and insights Nachiketa had gained. The young boy's journey and the wisdom he acquired became a source of inspiration for generations to come.

The story of the Katha Upanishad is a timeless narrative that delves into the deepest questions of human existence. Through the dialogue between Nachiketa and Yama, it imparts profound philosophical and spiritual teachings. The Upanishad emphasizes the impermanence of material pleasures, the immortality of the self, and the importance of pursuing wisdom over transient desires.

Nachiketa's journey is a metaphor for the seeker's quest for truth. It teaches that through patience, determination, and genuine inquiry, one can transcend the illusions of the material world and realize the eternal self. The Katha Upanishad continues to inspire and guide spiritual aspirants, offering a beacon of wisdom and enlightenment in the quest for the ultimate truth.

What Is Aum ?

The **Mandukya Upanishad** is one of the shortest yet most profound texts within the vast corpus of Upanishadic literature. Attached to the Atharva Veda, it consists of only twelve verses, but these concise teachings encapsulate the essence of the entire Vedic wisdom. This Upanishad is particularly significant in the study of Advaita Vedanta, a non-dualistic school of Indian philosophy. It addresses the nature of the self (Atman) and its relationship to the ultimate reality (Brahman), focusing on the sacred syllable "AUM" (or "OM") as the central theme. AUM is regarded as the primordial sound of the universe, representing the essence of all existence and the entire cosmos. The Upanishad's exploration of AUM and its breakdown into different states of consciousness provides a comprehensive framework for understanding the nature of reality and the path to spiritual enlightenment.

The Symbolism of AUM

The Mandukya Upanishad opens with an assertion of the supreme importance of AUM, declaring it to be the entirety of the universe. This syllable is not merely a sound but a symbol encompassing all aspects of existence. AUM is made up of three phonetic components: A, U, and M, each representing different dimensions of reality and states of consciousness. This tripartite structure serves as a powerful meditative tool that encapsulates the past, present, and future, and transcends them, pointing to the timeless and formless reality that underlies all phenomena. The significance of AUM in the Mandukya Upanishad is profound, as it is considered the key to unlocking the mysteries of the universe and the self.

AUM as the Whole Universe

"AUM, this word, is the whole universe. Its further explanation is the past, the present, and the future, everything is just AUM."

This verse emphasizes that AUM encompasses all that exists, including time and space. It is a holistic representation of the cosmos, signifying the totality of creation, maintenance, and dissolution. The sound of AUM vibrates through all aspects of life, embodying the essence of the universe's cyclical nature. Meditating on AUM allows one to align with this cosmic rhythm, transcending the limitations of individual existence to merge with the universal consciousness. This foundational concept sets the stage for the subsequent exploration of the states of consciousness and their deeper meanings.

The Four States of Consciousness

The heart of the Mandukya Upanishad lies in its exposition of the four states of consciousness: waking (Jagrat), dreaming (Swapna), deep sleep (Sushupti), and the transcendental state (Turiya). Each state is associated with a specific aspect of the syllable AUM, providing a framework for understanding the different levels of awareness and their implications for spiritual growth.

1. Waking State (Jagrat)

The waking state is symbolized by the sound "A" in AUM.

"The waking state, called Vaisvanara, is represented by the sound 'A'. It signifies the beginning and encompasses all."

In the waking state, individuals are conscious of the external world through their sensory organs. This state is characterized by an outward focus, where one engages with the physical environment and performs various activities. Vaisvanara, the deity associated with this state, represents the collective consciousness of all beings. The waking state is the most familiar to us, involving our daily interactions, work, and responsibilities. It is marked by the perception of diversity and multiplicity, as we navigate through the sensory experiences that define our reality. However, the Upanishad teaches that this state, while essential, is just the surface level of our consciousness.

2. Dreaming State (Swapna)

The dreaming state is symbolized by the sound "U" in AUM.

"The dreaming state, called Taijasa, is represented by the sound 'U'. It signifies superiority and is an intermediate state."

In the dreaming state, consciousness turns inward, and the mind creates an inner world of dreams. This state is characterized by the experiences of the dream world, which are vivid and real while they last but are fundamentally different from the waking state. Taijasa, the deity associated with the dreaming state, symbolizes the brilliance and activity of the mind. The dreaming state reveals the mind's capacity to generate its own reality, independent of the external world. It serves as a bridge between the waking state and the deeper state of consciousness, offering insights into the nature of mental processes and the subconscious mind. Dreams often reflect our thoughts, emotions, and unresolved issues, providing a mirror to our inner life.

3. Deep Sleep State (Sushupti)

The deep sleep state is symbolized by the sound "M" in AUM.

"The state of deep sleep, called Prajna, is represented by the sound 'M'. It signifies the merging or unifying aspect."

In the state of deep sleep, there is no awareness of the external or internal worlds. It is a state of undifferentiated consciousness, where the mind is in a state of rest and rejuvenation. Prajna, the deity associated with this state, represents profound wisdom and the unified experience of being. Deep sleep is marked by the absence of dreams and the dissolution of individual awareness into a state of potentiality. This state is essential for physical and mental restoration, as it allows the mind and body to recover from the activities of the waking and dreaming states. The experience of deep sleep suggests the presence of a deeper layer of consciousness that remains even when the mind is inactive.

4. Transcendental State (Turiya)

The fourth state is beyond the sounds of AUM and is represented by the silence that follows it.

"The fourth state is without parts, beyond all dealings, the end of phenomena, the auspicious, the non-dual."

Turiya is the transcendental state, beyond waking, dreaming, and deep sleep. It is the state of pure consciousness and ultimate reality, where the individual self (Atman) realizes its unity with Brahman. In Turiya, there is no duality, no subject-object distinction; it is the state of absolute peace and non-duality. This state is not experienced in the ordinary sense but is the underlying reality of all experiences. Turiya transcends the limitations of the previous three states, representing the true nature of the self. It is described as beyond empirical dealings, free from the play of phenomena, and characterized by auspiciousness and non-duality. Achieving Turiya involves realizing that the waking, dreaming, and deep sleep states are mere expressions of the same underlying consciousness.

AUM and the Realization of Brahman

The Mandukya Upanishad teaches that meditating on and understanding AUM can lead to the realization of Brahman, the ultimate reality. This realization involves transcending the three ordinary states of consciousness and experiencing Turiya, where the individual self merges with the universal self.

The Silence Beyond AUM

"This self is AUM, the indivisible syllable. Meditating on AUM, one realizes non-duality."

This verse emphasizes that AUM is not just a sound but a profound meditative practice. By focusing on AUM, one transcends the ordinary states of consciousness and realizes the non-dual nature of reality. This realization is the essence of Advaita Vedanta, the philosophy of non-duality, which teaches that the individual self and the universal self are one and the same. Meditating on AUM helps to quiet the mind, dissolve the ego, and reveal the underlying unity of all existence. This practice leads to a direct experience of the self's true nature, which is beyond the limitations of time, space, and causality.

Practical Implications of the Mandukya Upanishad

The teachings of the Mandukya Upanishad have profound practical implications for spiritual practice and daily life. By contemplating the nature of AUM and the states of consciousness, one can develop a deeper understanding of the self and the universe. This understanding helps in overcoming the illusions and attachments of the material world, leading to inner peace and spiritual liberation.

Meditative Practices

Meditation on AUM is a central practice derived from the Mandukya Upanishad. This meditation involves focusing on the sound and its components (A, U, M) and the silence that follows. Such meditation helps quiet the mind and facilitates the experience of the transcendental state (Turiya). By regularly practicing this form of meditation, individuals can cultivate a deeper awareness of their own consciousness and move towards the realization of their true nature. This practice also aids in developing concentration, reducing stress, and enhancing overall well-being.

Ethical Living

The Upanishad also emphasizes the importance of ethical living and self-discipline. By understanding the transient nature of the waking, dreaming, and deep sleep states, one can cultivate detachment from material desires and ego-driven actions. This detachment fosters a life of simplicity, purity, and inner peace. The realization that the self is beyond these states encourages individuals to live with integrity, compassion, and mindfulness. Ethical living involves adhering to principles such as truthfulness, non-violence, and self-restraint, which support spiritual growth and harmony with others.

Unity and Non-Duality

The realization of non-duality (Advaita) has profound implications for how we view ourselves and others. Understanding that all beings are manifestations of the same ultimate reality promotes compassion, empathy, and respect for all life. This perspective can transform personal relationships and societal interactions, fostering a sense of unity and harmony. By recognizing the interconnectedness of all existence, individuals can transcend the barriers of race, religion, and nationality, contributing to a more inclusive and peaceful world. The teachings of the Mandukya Upanishad inspire a vision of universal love and oneness, which can profoundly impact how we live and interact with others.

The Mandukya Upanishad, with its concise yet profound teachings, provides a pathway to understanding the nature of reality and the self. Its exploration of AUM and the four states of consciousness offers a comprehensive framework for spiritual practice and self-realization. Through meditation and contemplation, one can transcend the limitations of the physical and mental realms and experience the ultimate truth of non-dual consciousness.

By embracing the wisdom of the Mandukya Upanishad, seekers can embark on a journey of inner discovery, leading to the realization of their true nature as one with the infinite and eternal Brahman. This journey is not only about intellectual understanding but about direct experiential knowledge, which transforms one's perception of reality and brings about profound inner peace and spiritual liberation. The teachings of the Mandukya Upanishad encourage a life of simplicity, integrity, and compassion, grounded in the recognition of the interconnectedness of all existence. Through its profound insights, this ancient text continues to guide and inspire those seeking the ultimate truth and liberation.

Snake of Wisdom

The Yog Kundalini Upanishad begins with a philosophical discourse on the nature of the self and the universe. It emphasizes the importance of self-realization and the role of Kundalini Shakti in this process. The Upanishad explains that while every individual possesses this divine energy, it remains dormant due to ignorance and various impurities. Through dedicated practice and spiritual discipline, one can awaken this energy and realize their true nature.

This Upanishad also highlights the interconnectedness of all beings and the universe. It teaches that the same divine energy that flows through the cosmos also flows through each individual. By awakening Kundalini Shakti, one aligns their personal energy with the universal energy, leading to a state of harmony and unity with the divine.

Understanding of Kundalini Shakti

Kundalini Shakti is not just a concept but a profound reality experienced by yogis and spiritual practitioners. It is the primal energy of the universe, present in every individual. The Upanishad describes Kundalini Shakti as the creative force that manifests in the physical world as well as in the spiritual realm. In its dormant state, this energy lies coiled at the base of the spine, waiting to be awakened.

When awakened, Kundalini Shakti rises through the central channel of the subtle body, known as the Sushumna Nadi. This ascent is a process of purification and transformation, as the energy passes through the chakras, activating and energizing them. The journey of Kundalini Shakti is a journey of spiritual awakening, leading to higher states of consciousness and ultimate union with the divine.

The Dormant Energy and Its Awakening

The dormancy of Kundalini Shakti is due to various factors, including physical, mental, and spiritual blockages. These blockages can be in the form of negative emotions, unhealthy habits, or spiritual ignorance. The Upanishad teaches that through dedicated yogic practices, one can remove these blockages and prepare the body and mind for the awakening of Kundalini.

The awakening of Kundalini Shakti is often compared to the uncoiling of a serpent. This uncoiling is a gradual process, requiring patience, discipline, and the guidance of a knowledgeable guru. As Kundalini rises, it activates the chakras, leading to profound physical, mental, and spiritual transformations.

The Serpent Power and Its Symbolism

The serpent metaphor is rich in symbolism. It represents the latent potential within every individual, waiting to be awakened. The coiled serpent also symbolizes the cyclic nature of life and the continuous process of creation, preservation, and dissolution. When Kundalini Shakti awakens, it breaks the cycle of ignorance and leads to spiritual liberation.

The journey of Kundalini is not just about the ascent of energy but also about the transformation of consciousness. As the energy rises through the chakras, it purifies and activates them, leading to higher states of awareness and understanding. This process is a journey towards self-realization and union with the divine consciousness.

Seven Chakras

The Yog Kundalini Upanishad provides a comprehensive description of the seven chakras, their attributes, and the experiences associated with their activation. Each chakra represents a specific aspect of physical, emotional, and spiritual life.

Muladhara Chakra (Root Chakra)

The **Muladhara Chakra** is the foundation of the energy body. It is associated with the earth element, symbolizing stability and grounding. The activation of this chakra brings a sense of security and connection to the physical world. It helps in building a solid foundation for spiritual practice.

The journey of Kundalini begins at the Muladhara Chakra. As the energy awakens, it uncoils and starts its ascent, bringing about a profound transformation in the individual. The activation of the

Muladhara Chakra also involves the purification of the physical body, making it receptive to the higher energies.

Svadhisthana Chakra (Sacral Chakra)

The **Svadhisthana Chakra** governs creativity, sexuality, and the flow of emotions. It is associated with the water element, symbolizing fluidity and adaptability. The activation of this chakra brings about emotional purification and balance.

As Kundalini rises to the Svadhisthana Chakra, it releases suppressed desires and fears, allowing for a healthy expression of emotions. This chakra's activation enhances creativity and emotional intelligence, helping the individual to navigate their emotional life with greater ease and understanding.

Manipura Chakra (Solar Plexus Chakra)

The **Manipura Chakra** is associated with personal power, self-esteem, and willpower. It is linked to the fire element, representing transformation and energy. The activation of this chakra enhances one's sense of purpose and confidence.

When Kundalini reaches the Manipura Chakra, it transforms personal desires into spiritual aspirations. This chakra's activation provides the willpower and determination necessary for spiritual growth and self-mastery. It also involves the purification of the ego, leading to a greater sense of humility and inner strength.

Anahata Chakra (Heart Chakra)

The **Anahata Chakra** is associated with love, compassion, and emotional balance. It is linked to the air element, symbolizing freedom and expansiveness. The activation of this chakra opens the heart to deeper emotional connections and universal love.

As Kundalini rises to the Anahata Chakra, it awakens unconditional love and compassion. This chakra's activation bridges the gap between the lower and higher chakras, integrating physical, emotional, and spiritual aspects of the individual. It also involves the purification of the heart, leading to a greater sense of empathy and connectedness with others.

Vishuddha Chakra (Throat Chakra)

The **Vishuddha Chakra** governs communication, self-expression, and truth. It is associated with the ether element, representing purity and expansiveness. The activation of this chakra enhances one's ability to communicate effectively and express one's truth.

When Kundalini reaches the Vishuddha Chakra, it purifies speech and thought, promoting clarity and wisdom in communication. This chakra's activation also involves the purification of the mind, leading to greater intellectual and spiritual insight. It helps the individual to articulate their inner experiences and spiritual understanding with clarity and precision.

Ajna Chakra (Third Eye Chakra)

The **Ajna Chakra** is associated with intuition, insight, and higher perception. It is linked to the light element, symbolizing knowledge and clarity. The activation of this chakra enhances inner vision and intuitive understanding.

As Kundalini rises to the Ajna Chakra, it opens the inner eye, allowing the individual to perceive beyond the physical senses. This chakra's activation involves the purification of the mind and intellect, leading to a greater sense of inner knowing and spiritual insight. It helps the individual to connect with their higher self and access higher realms of consciousness.

Sahasrara Chakra (Crown Chakra)

The **Sahasrara Chakra** represents the highest state of consciousness and enlightenment. It is often depicted as a thousand-petaled lotus, symbolizing infinite possibilities. The activation of this chakra leads to the ultimate realization of unity with the divine.

When Kundalini reaches the Sahasrara Chakra, it brings about the ultimate realization of unity with the divine. This chakra's activation transcends all dualities and connects the individual self with the universal consciousness. It involves the purification of the entire being, leading to a state of pure awareness and spiritual liberation.

The Process of Kundalini Awakening

The Yog Kundalini Upanishad provides detailed instructions on the practices necessary for awakening Kundalini. These practices include various forms of yoga, pranayama, meditation, and the guidance of a knowledgeable guru. The awakening process can be gradual or sudden, depending on the practitioner's readiness and the removal of physical, emotional, and spiritual blockages.

Preparatory Practices

Before attempting to awaken Kundalini, it is essential to prepare the body and mind through regular yoga practice. This preparation includes:

- **Asanas (Postures):** Physical postures help in purifying the body and making it flexible, which is essential for the free flow of energy. Regular practice of asanas strengthens the body and removes physical blockages, making it conducive for the rise of Kundalini.

- **Pranayama (Breath Control):** Breathing exercises purify the nadis (energy channels) and increase the pranic energy, preparing the body for the rise of Kundalini. Pranayama helps in balancing the energy within the body and mind, creating a harmonious environment for spiritual growth.

- **Meditation:** Regular meditation practice calms the mind and helps in focusing on the inner journey. Meditation helps in developing concentration and inner awareness, essential for the safe and effective ascent of Kundalini.

- **Moral and Ethical Discipline:** Leading a life of purity, truthfulness, and self-discipline is crucial for Kundalini awakening. Ethical living helps in removing mental and emotional blockages, creating a pure and receptive mind for spiritual practices.

The Role of the Guru

The guidance of a knowledgeable and experienced guru is vital in the process of Kundalini awakening. The guru provides the necessary instructions, support, and protection to the disciple, ensuring a safe and effective awakening process. The guru also helps in removing spiritual blockages and provides the necessary guidance for the individual's spiritual journey.

The Yog Kundalini Upanishad offers a comprehensive guide to understanding and awakening Kundalini Shakti. Through its teachings on the seven chakras, the preparatory practices, and the role of the guru, it provides a roadmap for spiritual seekers to achieve higher states of consciousness and self-realization. The awakening of Kundalini is a transformative process that not only enhances physical and mental well-being but also leads to the ultimate goal of union with the divine consciousness. This Upanishad remains a vital text for those on the path of yoga and spiritual awakening, offering timeless wisdom and guidance.

By elaborating on these sections and including detailed explanations, personal experiences, and practical insights, you can create a comprehensive 10,000-word document on the Yog Kundalini Upanishad, Kundalini Shakti, and the seven chakras.

Six Questions Of Existence

The **Prashna Upanishad** is a revered text within the Atharva **Veda** that explores profound spiritual and metaphysical questions through a structured dialogue between the sage Pippalada and six dedicated seekers. Each question posed by these seekers addresses fundamental aspects of existence, consciousness, and the ultimate purpose of life. The responses from Pippalada offer deep insights into Vedic philosophy, emphasizing the interconnectedness of the physical and spiritual realms.

Story: The Seekers and the Sage

In ancient times, there were six young students named **Sukesha, Satyakama, Gargya, Kausalya, Bhargava,** and **Kabandhi**. They were deeply curious about the mysteries of life and existence. Hearing of the renowned sage Pippalada, known for his profound wisdom and spiritual knowledge, they set out on a journey to seek his guidance.

Upon reaching Pippalada's tranquil hermitage, nestled amidst nature's serenity, the students approached him with humility and reverence. They expressed their earnest desire to learn from him and unravel the profound truths that lay beyond the surface of daily existence. Recognizing their sincerity and thirst for knowledge, Pippalada welcomed them warmly into his abode.

Understanding that true wisdom requires both intellectual understanding and spiritual purification, Pippalada prescribed a year of rigorous discipline for his students. During this transformative period, the six students immersed themselves in austere practices, cultivating inner stillness and strength through meditation, self-restraint, and devotion to their studies.

Under Pippalada's compassionate guidance, the students delved deep into the scriptures, contemplating the ancient teachings that elucidated the nature of the self, the universe, and the ultimate reality. They learned not only from Pippalada's words but also from his way of life—a life attuned to the rhythms of nature and steeped in profound spiritual awareness.

As the year drew to a close, Pippalada observed the transformation in his students. Their minds were clearer, their hearts more open, and their spirits attuned to the subtle vibrations of the cosmos. Sensing their readiness, Pippalada invited them to pose their questions, knowing that their inquiries would be not mere intellectual curiosity but profound quests for truth and understanding.

The First Question: The Origin of Creation

Kabandhi Katyayana posed the first question about the origin of all created beings. Pippalada explained that in the beginning, **Prajapati**, the lord of creation, desired offspring and created a pair: **matter (Rayi)** and **life force (Prana)**. From this primordial pair emerged all creatures. Pippalada elaborated that Prana, the vital life force, and Rayi, the material substance, are interdependent. Prana animates beings and sustains life, while Rayi provides the physical form. This duality is the foundation of all creation, and their interplay maintains the universe.

Prajapati's act of creation is described as a cosmic process where Rayi and Prana together bring forth the diversity of life. Pippalada highlighted the sun as the embodiment of Prana, symbolizing the life-giving energy that sustains all beings. The moon, associated with Rayi, represents the material aspects of creation, including fertility and growth. This dynamic relationship between Prana and Rayi illustrates the balance between the spiritual and material worlds, underscoring the interconnectedness of all life forms.

The Second Question: The Powers that Sustain the Body

The second question, posed by Bhargava, the son of Vaidarbhi, inquired about the various powers that sustain the body and which among them is supreme. Pippalada explained that several deities or forces operate within the human body, including **speech (Vāk)**, **sight (Chakshus)**, **hearing (Shravana)**, **mind (Manas)**, and **breath (Prana)**. These faculties work together to maintain life, but among them, Prana is supreme. To illustrate this, Pippalada narrated a story where the senses—speech, sight, hearing, mind, and Prana—debated their relative importance. Each sense claimed supremacy, but when Prana decided to withdraw, all other senses began to fail, demonstrating that Prana is the most crucial and fundamental power sustaining life.

This story underscores the indispensability of Prana. While other faculties are essential for specific functions, Prana is the foundational life force without which the body cannot survive. It supports all physiological processes and keeps the body functioning. This teaching highlights the importance of breath control and the practice of **Pranayama (breath regulation)** in yoga as a means to harness and balance this vital life force, ensuring overall health and well-being.

The Third Question: The Nature and Functions of Prana

Kausalya, the son of Asvalayana, asked the third question about the origin of Prana and its functions within the body. Pippalada explained that Prana is born from the **Self (Atman)** and is nourished by food. He described how Prana distributes itself into five forms within the body: **Prana (the upward-moving breath), Apana (the downward-moving breath), Samana (the breath that governs digestion and assimilation), Udana (the breath that moves upwards and governs the function of the mind during sleep and at the time of death)**, and **Vyana (the breath that circulates throughout the body)**. Each form of Prana has a distinct role, ensuring the proper functioning and health of the body. This division highlights the comprehensive and essential role of Prana in sustaining life.

- Prana, the upward-moving breath, resides in the head and

governs respiration and sensory perception.

- Apana, the downward-moving breath, is located in the lower abdomen and is responsible for excretion and reproductive functions.
- Samana, residing in the stomach, is crucial for digestion and the assimilation of nutrients.
- Udana, moving upwards, is associated with speech, the movement of energy during sleep, and the journey of the soul after death.
- Vyana, which pervades the entire body, regulates circulation and the distribution of energy.

This detailed explanation shows how Prana, in its various forms, is central to maintaining the body's balance and health.

The Fourth Question: The Role of Sleep, Dreams, and Waking States

Sauryayani Gargya asked the fourth question concerning the different states of consciousness: waking, dreaming, and deep sleep. Pippalada explained that during the waking state, the mind and senses are active and engage with the external world, gathering experiences and knowledge. In the dream state, the mind creates its own world using the impressions and memories of the waking state, offering a unique form of perception and reality. In the state of deep sleep, the mind withdraws into the Self, experiencing a state of bliss and rest. This state represents a temporary return to the source of all consciousness, where there is no awareness of the external world or the individual self. Upon waking, the individual re-engages with the world through the mind and senses, continuing the cycle of experiences.

- In the waking state, the Atman (Self) is fully engaged with the external world through the mind and senses. This state is characterized by activity and interaction with the physical environment.
- In the dream state, the Atman experiences a world created by the mind, reflecting the desires, fears, and impressions accumulated during the waking state. Dreams offer insights into the subconscious mind and its workings.
- In the deep sleep state, the Atman retreats into itself, experiencing a state of pure being and bliss. This state is devoid of any duality or mental activity, representing a return to the source.
- The transition between these states highlights the dynamic nature of consciousness and the interplay between the mind and the Self.

The Fifth Question: Meditation on Om and its Importance

Satyakama, son of Sibi, inquired about the significance of the sacred syllable **Om** and its relation to the states of consciousness. Pippalada explained that Om is the symbol of the ultimate reality, **Brahman**. It encapsulates the entire universe and the three states of consciousness—waking (**A**), dreaming (**U**), and deep sleep (**M**). By meditating on Om, one can transcend these states and realize the Self (Atman), ultimately achieving union with Brahman. Om serves as a powerful tool for meditation, guiding the practitioner towards spiritual enlightenment and the realization of the ultimate truth. It represents the eternal sound, the cosmic vibration underlying all existence.

- The sound 'A' represents the waking state, where consciousness is outwardly directed and engaged with the external world.
- The sound 'U' symbolizes the dreaming state, where consciousness is turned inward, experiencing the subtle, mental world.
- The sound 'M' signifies the deep sleep state, where consciousness is in a state of rest and unity with the Self.

Meditating on the entirety of Om (A-U-M) leads to the transcendence of these three states and the realization of **Turiya**, the fourth state, which is pure consciousness and the essence of Brahman. Om thus acts as a bridge between the individual self and the supreme reality, aiding the practitioner in their journey towards enlightenment.

The Sixth Question: The Ultimate Goal of Life and Liberation

The final question is asked by Sukesha, son of Bharadvaja, who seeks knowledge about the Purusha, the supreme being, and the ultimate goal of life. Pippalada explains that Purusha is the inner self, the eternal witness, and the ultimate cause of all creation. Realizing the Purusha leads to liberation (moksha), the highest aim of human existence. This realization involves understanding the true nature of the Self, which is beyond birth and death, eternal and unchanging. By knowing the Self, one transcends the cycle of samsara (birth and death) and attains a state of ultimate freedom and bliss.

Pippalada describes the Purusha as the indwelling spirit that resides within all beings, the eternal witness that observes all actions without attachment. This Purusha is the source of all life and consciousness, beyond the limitations of time and space. Realizing the Purusha involves a deep, intuitive understanding of one's true nature, beyond the physical body and the mind. It is the recognition that the individual self (Atman) is identical with the universal Self (Brahman). This knowledge liberates one from the bondage of karma and the cycle of rebirth, leading to a state of eternal bliss and union with the divine.

The Prashna Upanishad concludes with Pippalada blessing the six seekers, who are now satisfied with the profound wisdom they have received. The sage's teachings have illuminated the path to spiritual understanding, emphasizing the importance of self-realization, the nature of Prana, the significance of Om, and the ultimate goal of liberation. Through disciplined practice, devotion, and the guidance of a knowledgeable teacher, one can attain the profound knowledge necessary for spiritual liberation. This Upanishad offers timeless wisdom, guiding seekers on their spiritual journey and helping them understand the deeper truths of existence.

The Prashna Upanishad, with its exploration of vital questions about life, consciousness, and the ultimate reality, serves as a guide for spiritual aspirants. It teaches that the journey to self-realization requires a harmonious balance of physical, mental, and spiritual disciplines. The interplay of Prana and Rayi, the functions of the different forms of Prana, the states of consciousness, the significance of Om, and the realization of the Purusha are all integral aspects of this profound journey. The teachings of the Prashna Upanishad continue to inspire and enlighten seekers of truth, providing a roadmap to the ultimate goal of liberation.

The teachings of the Prashna Upanishad emphasize the unity of the physical and spiritual aspects of existence. The seekers, through their questions, explore the nature of life, the fundamental forces that sustain the body, the various states of consciousness, the significance of sacred symbols, and the ultimate goal of life. Pippalada's responses are rich with metaphysical insights, illustrating the profound wisdom embedded in Vedic philosophy. The Upanishad underscores the importance of understanding the interconnectedness of all aspects of existence and realizing the Self's unity with the supreme reality, Brahman.

In conclusion, the Prashna Upanishad serves as a profound guide for those seeking deeper understanding and spiritual enlightenment. It addresses essential questions about life, consciousness, and the ultimate purpose of existence, providing timeless wisdom that continues to inspire and guide spiritual seekers on their journey toward self-realization and liberation. The dialogues between Pippalada and the six seekers highlight the importance of discipline, devotion, and the guidance of a wise teacher in the pursuit of spiritual knowledge. Through its exploration of the fundamental aspects of existence, the Prashna Upanishad offers valuable insights into the nature of reality and the path to spiritual liberation.

Sound Of Universe

The **Nādabindu Upanishad** is a profound and spiritually significant text within the corpus of Upanishadic literature. Associated with the Rig Veda, it is a minor Upanishad that delves deeply into the practices and philosophies of yoga and meditation. The term "Nādabindu" is derived from two Sanskrit words: "Nāda," meaning sound, and "Bindu," meaning point or dot. Together, they refer to the point where the primordial sound (Nāda) manifests and symbolizes the union of individual consciousness with the universal consciousness.

The primary focus of the Nādabindu Upanishad is Nāda Yoga, the yoga of sound. It emphasizes the importance of inner sound in the practice of meditation and spiritual development. The text explores the significance of Nāda, the inner sound that yogis hear during deep meditation, and how it can lead to the ultimate realization of the self.

The Concept of Nāda

Nāda is described as the primal sound or vibration from which the entire universe originates. In the context of yoga, Nāda refers to the inner sound that becomes perceptible to the practitioner during deep meditation. This sound is said to be heard in the right ear and can range from subtle hums to more distinct musical tones.

Understanding Nāda

In the Upanishadic tradition, Nāda is considered the sound of the universe, the vibration that underlies all creation. It is the sonic representation of the divine, the auditory manifestation of the absolute. Just as all physical forms are expressions of Brahman, the ultimate reality, Nāda is the sound form of Brahman. Meditating on Nāda is believed to purify the mind and senses, paving the way for higher states of consciousness. Nāda is not merely an external sound but an internal, spiritual experience. As practitioners deepen their meditation, they shift their focus from external auditory stimuli to the internal, spiritual sound. This internal sound is believed to be more subtle and profound, leading the practitioner to higher states of awareness and eventually to self-realization.

The Bindu and Its Significance

Bindu, meaning point or dot, represents the point of origin and convergence in the Nādabindu Upanishad. It signifies the ultimate reality or the source from which all creation emanates. In the practice of Nāda Yoga, Bindu symbolizes the focal point of meditation where the practitioner's consciousness merges with the sound.

The Symbolism of Bindu

The concept of Bindu is rich with symbolism. In various spiritual traditions, Bindu is seen as the point where creation begins and ends. It is the source of all energy and the point of ultimate concentration. In the context of the Nādabindu Upanishad, Bindu represents the point of ultimate spiritual realization, where the individual consciousness merges with the universal consciousness.

This point is often associated with the Ajna Chakra, the third eye center, which is considered the seat of intuition and higher wisdom. By meditating on the Bindu, practitioners aim to transcend the limitations of the individual self and experience the universal consciousness.

The Practice of Nāda Yoga

The Nādabindu Upanishad outlines the practice of Nāda Yoga, which involves meditating on the inner sound. This practice is divided into several stages:

Purification

Before beginning the practice of Nāda Yoga, it is essential to purify the body and mind through the practice of asanas (postures) and pranayama (breath control). This helps to remove physical and mental blockages, making it easier to concentrate on the inner sound.

The Role of Asanas and Pranayama

Asanas, or physical postures, play a crucial role in preparing the body for meditation. By practicing asanas, the body becomes flexible and strong, allowing the practitioner to sit comfortably for extended periods. This physical stability is essential for maintaining focus during meditation. Pranayama, or breath control, is equally important. Through pranayama, practitioners learn to control their breath, which in turn helps to calm the mind. Techniques such as Nadi Shodhana (alternate nostril breathing) and Ujjayi (victorious breath) are particularly effective in preparing the mind for meditation. By harmonizing the breath, practitioners create a state of inner balance and tranquility, which is conducive to experiencing Nāda.

Concentration on External Sounds

The initial stage involves focusing on external sounds. This could be the chanting of mantras, the sound of a bell, or any other soothing sound. The purpose of this stage is to train the mind to become aware of and concentrate on sound.

The Use of Mantras and External Sounds

Mantras are sacred sounds or phrases that are repeated during meditation to help focus the mind. The use of mantras, such as "Om," creates a vibrational frequency that aligns with the inner sound of Nāda. By chanting mantras, practitioners begin to tune their awareness to the subtler aspects of sound.

External sounds, like the ringing of a bell or the sound of a flute, serve as auditory anchors that help draw the mind inward. These sounds are used to develop the ability to concentrate on a single point of focus. As practitioners become more proficient in focusing on external sounds, they gradually shift their attention to the internal sound of Nāda.

Listening to the Inner Sound

As the practice deepens, the practitioner shifts their focus from external sounds to the inner sound, or Nāda. This sound is perceived internally, often in the right ear, and becomes the focal point of meditation.

The Transition to Internal Sound

The transition from external to internal sound marks a significant shift in the practice of Nāda Yoga. This stage requires heightened concentration and a refined sense of hearing. The inner sound, or Nāda, may initially appear as a faint hum or a subtle tone. With continued practice, this sound becomes more pronounced and distinct. Practitioners are encouraged to maintain a relaxed yet attentive state of mind, allowing the inner sound to arise naturally. By focusing on Nāda, the mind gradually becomes absorbed in the sound, leading to deeper states of meditation. This process of absorption is known as Pratyahara, the withdrawal of the senses, which is a crucial step in achieving higher states of consciousness.

Merging with the Sound

With continued practice, the practitioner becomes more attuned to the inner sound. The mind becomes absorbed in Nāda, leading to deep states of meditation. The ultimate goal is to merge with the sound, transcending the individual self and experiencing the unity of all existence.

The Experience of Samadhi

The merging with Nāda culminates in the experience of Samadhi, a state of meditative absorption where the practitioner transcends the limitations of the individual self. In Samadhi, the distinction between the meditator and the object of meditation dissolves. The practitioner experiences a profound sense of unity with the inner sound and, by extension, with the universal consciousness.

This state of oneness is characterized by a deep sense of peace, bliss, and expanded awareness. The realization that the self is not separate from the universe but an integral part of it marks the pinnacle of Nāda Yoga practice.

Stages of Nāda

The Nādabindu Upanishad describes four stages of Nāda that the practitioner may experience during deep meditation:

Vaikhari

This is the grossest stage of Nāda and is perceived as a loud and distinct sound, often similar to the sound of a bell or a conch shell. At this stage, the mind is still relatively externalized.

Characteristics of Vaikhari

In the Vaikhari stage, the sound is loud and clear, making it easy for practitioners to focus their attention. This stage is essential for beginners as it helps them develop the ability to concentrate on sound. The distinct nature of Vaikhari allows practitioners to anchor their awareness, making it easier to transition to subtler stages of Nāda. The sounds experienced in this stage are often associated with the physical world, and the mind is still engaged with sensory perceptions. However, as practitioners deepen their focus, the external distractions begin to fade, paving the way for more refined experiences of Nāda.

Madhyama

The sound becomes subtler and more internalized. It is often described as the humming of bees or the sound of a flute. The mind begins to turn inward, and concentration deepens.

The Subtleties of Madhyama

In the Madhyama stage, the inner sound becomes more subtle and refined. The distinct loudness of Vaikhari gives way to a softer, more melodic tone. This stage marks a deeper level of concentration, where the mind becomes more absorbed in the internal sound.

The sounds experienced in Madhyama are less tied to the physical world and more reflective of the inner landscape of the mind. The practitioner's awareness becomes more internalized, reducing the influence of external stimuli. This stage is crucial for developing a deeper sense of inner calm and focus.

Pashyanti

The sound is very subtle, resembling the sound of a drum or a lute. At this stage, the practitioner experiences profound inner silence and stillness.

The Depth of Pashyanti

The Pashyanti stage represents a significant shift towards inner stillness and silence. The sound becomes very subtle, almost blending with the background of inner silence. The practitioner's mind reaches a state of profound calm, free from the distractions of the external world.

In this stage, the experience of Nāda becomes more abstract and less tied to specific sounds. The practitioner begins to perceive the sound as an expression of the underlying silence, leading to a deeper understanding of the nature of reality. The inner silence of Pashyanti paves the way for the ultimate experience of unity in the Para stage.

Para

This is the subtlest and most refined stage of Nāda. The sound is extremely faint, almost imperceptible, and is often described as the sound of silence. At this stage, the practitioner experiences complete unity with the sound and the universal consciousness.

The Unity of Para

The Para stage represents the pinnacle of Nāda Yoga practice. The sound is extremely subtle, blending seamlessly with the experience of inner silence. In this stage, the practitioner experiences a profound sense of unity with the inner sound and, by extension, with the universal consciousness. The distinction between sound and silence dissolves, leading to the realization that they are two aspects of the same reality. This experience of unity transcends the limitations of the individual self, allowing the practitioner to experience the oneness of all existence. The Para stage is characterized by a profound sense of peace, bliss, and expanded awareness.

Benefits of Nāda Yoga

The practice of Nāda Yoga as described in the Nādabindu

Upanishad offers numerous benefits, both physical and spiritual:

Mental Clarity

Concentration on the inner sound helps to quiet the mind and reduce mental chatter, leading to increased mental clarity and focus.

Enhancing Mental Clarity

By focusing on Nāda, practitioners can achieve a state of mental clarity that is difficult to attain through other means. The practice of Nāda Yoga helps to quiet the incessant chatter of the mind, allowing practitioners to experience a state of inner calm and focus. This clarity of mind is essential for making informed decisions and approaching life's challenges with a clear and balanced perspective.

Emotional Balance

By meditating on Nāda, practitioners can release suppressed emotions and achieve greater emotional stability and balance.

Achieving Emotional Balance

The practice of Nāda Yoga helps to release suppressed emotions, leading to greater emotional balance and stability. By focusing on the inner sound, practitioners can bring unresolved emotions to the surface and release them in a healthy and constructive manner. This process of emotional release is essential for achieving a state of inner peace and harmony.

Spiritual Insight

Nāda Yoga opens the doorway to higher states of consciousness, allowing practitioners to gain deeper spiritual insights and understanding.

Gaining Spiritual Insight

The practice of Nāda Yoga opens the doorway to higher states of consciousness, allowing practitioners to gain deeper spiritual insights and understanding. By meditating on Nāda, practitioners can experience the unity of all existence and gain a deeper understanding of the nature of reality. This spiritual insight is essential for achieving self-realization and experiencing the ultimate goal of Nāda Yoga.

Self-Realization

The ultimate goal of Nāda Yoga is self-realization, where the individual self merges with the universal consciousness, leading to a profound sense of unity and enlightenment.

Achieving Self-Realization

The ultimate goal of Nāda Yoga is self-realization, where the individual self merges with the universal consciousness. This state of unity is characterized by a profound sense of peace, bliss, and expanded awareness. By meditating on Nāda, practitioners can transcend the limitations of the individual self and experience the oneness of all existence.

The Role of the Guru

The Nādabindu Upanishad emphasizes the importance of the guidance of a guru in the practice of Nāda Yoga. A knowledgeable and experienced guru can provide the necessary instructions, support, and protection to ensure a safe and effective practice. The guru helps the disciple to navigate the various stages of Nāda and offers guidance on how to overcome obstacles and challenges.

The guidance of a guru is essential for the practice of Nāda Yoga. A knowledgeable and experienced guru can provide the necessary instructions, support, and protection to ensure a safe and effective practice. The guru helps the disciple to navigate the various stages of

Nāda and offers guidance on how to overcome obstacles and challenges. In the practice of Nāda Yoga, the role of the guru is crucial. The guru provides the necessary guidance and support to help the disciple navigate the various stages of Nāda. The guru also offers protection and support to ensure a safe and effective practice. By following the guidance of a guru, practitioners can achieve the ultimate goal of self-realization.

The Significance of Silence

Silence plays a crucial role in the practice of Nāda Yoga. The Upanishad teaches that true sound can only be perceived in silence. By cultivating inner and outer silence, practitioners can become more attuned to the subtle inner sound. Silence helps to quiet the mind and create a conducive environment for deep meditation.

The Role of Silence in Nāda Yoga

Silence plays a crucial role in the practice of Nāda Yoga. By cultivating inner and outer silence, practitioners can become more attuned to the subtle inner sound. Silence helps to quiet the mind and create a conducive environment for deep meditation. The Upanishad teaches that true sound can only be perceived in silence.

The Practice of Silence

In the practice of Nāda Yoga, silence is essential. By creating a state of inner and outer silence, practitioners can become more attuned to the subtle inner sound. This state of silence helps to quiet the mind and create a conducive environment for deep meditation. The practice of silence is essential for achieving the ultimate goal of self-realization.

The Symbolism of Sound and Silence

In the Nādabindu Upanishad, sound and silence are seen as complementary aspects of the same reality. Sound represents the manifest world, while silence represents the unmanifest, the source from which all sound arises. By meditating on Nāda, practitioners experience the unity of sound and silence, leading to the realization of the non-dual nature of reality.

The Unity of Sound and Silence

The Nādabindu Upanishad teaches that sound and silence are complementary aspects of the same reality. Sound represents the manifest world, while silence represents the unmanifest, the source from which all sound arises. By meditating on Nāda, practitioners experience the unity of sound and silence, leading to the realization of the non-dual nature of reality.

The Non-Dual Nature of Reality

The practice of Nāda Yoga helps practitioners to realize the non-dual nature of reality. By meditating on Nāda, practitioners experience the unity of sound and silence, leading to the realization that they are two aspects of the same reality. This realization is essential for achieving self-realization and experiencing the ultimate goal of Nāda Yoga.

The Ultimate Goal of Nāda Yoga

The ultimate goal of Nāda Yoga, as described in the Nādabindu Upanishad, is to transcend the limitations of the individual self and merge with the universal consciousness. This state of unity is characterized by a profound sense of peace, bliss, and enlightenment. It is the realization of the oneness of all existence and the experience of the self as part of the infinite and eternal reality.

The State of Unity

The ultimate goal of Nāda Yoga is to transcend the limitations of the individual self and merge with the universal consciousness. This state of unity is characterized by a profound sense of peace, bliss, and enlightenment. By meditating on Nāda, practitioners can experience the oneness of all existence and realize their true nature as part of the infinite and eternal reality.

The Experience of Bliss

The experience of unity in Nāda Yoga is characterized by a profound sense of bliss. This state of bliss arises from the realization that the self is not separate from the universe but an integral part of it. By merging with the universal consciousness, practitioners experience a state of complete contentment and joy.

The Nādabindu Upanishad provides a profound exploration of the practice of Nāda Yoga, emphasizing the importance of inner sound in the journey of self-realization. Through the stages of purification, concentration, and meditation on Nāda, practitioners can achieve higher states of consciousness and ultimately realize their true nature. The guidance of a guru, the cultivation of silence, and the understanding of the symbolism of sound and silence are essential aspects of this practice. The Nādabindu Upanishad remains a timeless and invaluable text for those seeking to explore the depths of their inner world and experience the unity of all existence through the practice of Nāda Yoga.

By understanding and practicing the teachings of the Nādabindu Upanishad, individuals can embark on a profound spiritual journey that leads to self-realization and the ultimate experience of oneness with the universe. The text offers a detailed roadmap for practitioners, guiding them through the various stages of Nāda Yoga and providing insights into the deeper aspects of sound and silence. Through dedicated practice and the guidance of a guru, individuals can achieve a state of unity and enlightenment, realizing their true nature as part of the infinite and eternal reality.

What Is That Knowing Which All This Becomes Known?

The **Mundaka Upanishad** is one of the primary Upanishads and belongs to the Atharva Veda. The term "Mundaka" is derived from "mund," meaning "to shave" in Sanskrit, symbolizing the shedding of ignorance through the knowledge of the ultimate truth. The text is structured in a poetic and philosophical form, and it provides a clear and systematic exposition of the nature of the ultimate reality (Brahman), the means to realize it, and the distinction between higher knowledge (para vidya) and lower knowledge (apara vidya). The Upanishad is divided into three mundakas (sections), each further subdivided into khandas (parts).

Story of Shaunak and Maharshi Angira

The Mundaka Upanishad begins with a dialogue between a great householder named Shaunak and the sage Maharshi Angira. Shaunak

underscores the unique and all-encompassing nature of Brahman.

To elucidate the profound and abstract nature of Brahman, Maharshi Angira employs several metaphors that convey its essence in a relatable manner. One of the prominent metaphors used is that of a spider.

The spider weaves its web from its own substance and eventually withdraws the web back into itself. This metaphor illustrates that the universe is created from Brahman, sustained by it, and ultimately dissolves back into Brahman. Just as the web is a part of the spider, the universe is an extension of Brahman's own being.

Another metaphor compares Brahman to fire and sparks. The fire represents Brahman, and the sparks symbolize the individual souls (jivas). Each spark emerges from the fire, possessing its essence, yet maintains a distinct identity. Similarly, individual souls originate from Brahman, reflecting its divine essence while experiencing a unique existence. This metaphor highlights the interconnectedness of all beings with the supreme reality and their inherent divinity.

The Process of Creation

The Mundaka Upanishad provides a detailed account of the process of creation, emphasizing that everything originates from Brahman. It describes how the universe unfolds in a systematic manner, starting from the highest reality and descending into the material world. According to the Upanishad, Brahman first manifests as Hiranyagarbha, the golden womb or cosmic egg, which contains the potential for all creation. From Hiranyagarbha emerges the primal elements (mahabhutas) and the various deities that govern the natural forces. These elements combine to form the physical universe, including the earth, sky, and all living beings.

This hierarchical process of creation underscores the interconnectedness of all existence and highlights the ultimate unity of everything in Brahman. It also emphasizes that the material world, while real in its own domain, is ultimately dependent on the higher reality of Brahman.

The Path to Self-Realization

Maharshi Angira outlines the path to self-realization, emphasizing the importance of inner purification, ethical conduct, and spiritual practice. The Upanishad stresses that true knowledge is not merely intellectual understanding but a direct and experiential realization of the self and its oneness with Brahman.

The path to self-realization involves several key stages:

- **Ethical Living**: The foundation of spiritual practice is ethical living, which includes truthfulness, non-violence, self-control, and compassion. These virtues purify the mind and create a conducive environment for higher knowledge.

- **Renunciation**: The seeker is encouraged to renounce attachment to material possessions and desires. This renunciation is not necessarily physical but involves a mental detachment from worldly pleasures and distractions.

- **Meditation and Contemplation**: Meditation and contemplation are essential practices for attaining self-realization. Through deep meditation, the seeker transcends the limitations of the mind and senses and experiences the true nature of the self.

- **Knowledge of the Self**: The ultimate goal is the realization of the self as identical to Brahman. This realization brings about a profound transformation in one's perception and understanding of reality, leading to liberation from the cycle of birth and death.

The Role of the Guru

The Upanishad emphasizes the importance of the guru (spiritual teacher) in the journey to self-realization. The guru, having attained self-knowledge, can illuminate the path for the disciple, helping to overcome obstacles and misconceptions. The relationship between the guru and the disciple is based on trust, respect, and dedication.

The guru imparts wisdom through teachings, personal example, and direct transmission of spiritual energy. The disciple, in turn, must approach the guru with humility, sincerity, and an open heart. This relationship is crucial for the seeker's spiritual growth and understanding.

The Symbolism of the Two Birds

One of the most profound metaphors in the Mundaka Upanishad is the symbolism of the two birds. The Upanishad describes two birds sitting on the same tree. One bird eats the sweet and bitter fruits of the tree, while the other bird merely watches without partaking.

The two birds represent the individual self (jivatman) and the supreme self (paramatman). The bird that eats the fruits symbolizes the jivatman, which experiences the pleasures and pains of the material world. The bird that watches symbolizes the paramatman, which remains detached and unaffected by worldly experiences.

This metaphor highlights the dual aspects of existence and the importance of recognizing the higher self within. By identifying with the paramatman, one can transcend the limitations of the jivatman and realize the true nature of the self as Brahman.

The Unity of Knowledge and Action

The Mundaka Upanishad emphasizes the unity of knowledge (jnana) and action (karma). It teaches that true knowledge is not separate from righteous action. Ethical conduct and selfless service are integral to the path of self-realization.

The Upanishad asserts that actions performed with a pure heart and a sense of devotion lead to the purification of the mind and the realization of the self. It emphasizes that knowledge without action is incomplete, and action without knowledge is blind. The integration of knowledge and action is essential for attaining liberation.

The Ultimate Goal: Liberation (Moksha)

The ultimate goal of the teachings in the Mundaka Upanishad is liberation (moksha). Liberation is described as the state of ultimate freedom and transcendence, where one realizes the true nature of the self and its oneness with Brahman. It is the state of eternal bliss, free from the cycles of birth and death.

The Upanishad teaches that liberation is attained through the realization of the self and the direct experience of Brahman. This realization brings about a profound transformation in one's perception and understanding of reality, leading to inner peace, freedom, and infinite bliss.

The Mundaka Upanishad offers a profound and comprehensive exploration of the nature of the self, the universe, and the ultimate reality known as Brahman. Through its poetic and philosophical teachings, the Upanishad provides a clear and systematic guide to the path of self-realization and liberation.

It emphasizes the importance of ethical living, the role of the guru, the practice of meditation, and the integration of knowledge and action. By realizing the true nature of the self and its oneness with Brahman, one can transcend the limitations of the material world and attain liberation.

The teachings of the Mundaka Upanishad continue to inspire and guide spiritual seekers on their journey towards self-realization and ultimate truth. Its timeless wisdom and profound insights remain relevant and valuable in the modern age, offering a path to inner peace, freedom, and infinite bliss.

Everything Belongs To Him

The **Taittiriya Upanishad,** a significant text within the Vedic tradition, is embedded within the Yajurveda, specifically the Taittiriya school of this Veda. Comprising three chapters, or Adhyayas, it is a Mukhya (principal) Upanishad, composed around the 6th century BCE. The Taittiriya Upanishad holds a distinguished place in the corpus of Vedic literature, reflecting the profound philosophical inquiries of ancient Indian sages.

The Yajurveda, one of the four Vedas, primarily deals with the procedures for rituals and sacrifices. Within it, the Taittiriya Upanishad forms a part of the "Krishna" (black) Yajurveda, distinguished from the "Shukla" (white) Yajurveda by its unarranged and motley collection of verses. The term "Taittiriya" is derived from Tittiri, either referring to the sage Tittiri, a pupil of Yaska, or mythically from students who transformed into partridges to gain wisdom.

Significance and Philosophical Themes

The Taittiriya Upanishad is revered for its exploration of profound metaphysical concepts such as the nature of Brahman (the ultimate reality), Atman (the Self), and the interrelationship between the microcosm (individual) and the macrocosm (universe). It presents a holistic vision of life that integrates spiritual wisdom with practical ethical guidelines, making it a foundational text for understanding the core principles of Vedanta philosophy.

Shiksha Valli

The Shiksha Valli is the first chapter of the Taittiriya Upanishad, focusing on the education and ethical training of students in the Vedic tradition. The term "Shiksha" translates to "instruction" or "education," reflecting the chapter's emphasis on the foundational aspects of learning. This section comprises twelve Anuvakas (lessons) that guide students through various stages of their educational journey, from initiation to graduation.

The first lesson begins with benedictions and prayers, establishing a sacred and auspicious beginning for the students. It emphasizes the importance of speaking the truth and righteousness, invoking protection and blessings from Brahman for both the student and the teacher. This initial invocation sets the tone for the holistic and ethical education that follows.

The second lesson introduces the significance of phonetics, asserting that mastering the principles of sound is crucial for Vedic studies. It details the structure of vowels, consonants, and the correct pronunciation of Vedic texts, highlighting the importance of linguistic precision. The third lesson extends this by exploring the interconnectedness of all elements in the universe, using the metaphor of speech as the link between different parts of the body and the cosmos.

In the fourth lesson, the teacher prays for an influx of eager and disciplined students, emphasizing the role of the teacher in guiding and inspiring learners. The lesson underscores the ethical responsibilities of both teachers and students, promoting a disciplined and respectful learning environment.

The fifth lesson discusses the sacred syllables "Bhur," "Bhuvah," and "Svar," associating them with different aspects of breath and life. It also introduces the concept of Brahman as the ultimate reality, asserting the oneness of all existence. The sixth lesson elaborates on the characteristics of the Self that align with Brahman, encouraging meditation and Self-realization as paths to understanding this oneness.

The seventh lesson presents the idea of parallelism in knowledge, suggesting that the principles governing the macrocosm (universe) and the microcosm (individual) are interconnected. It highlights the fractal nature of existence, where the same fundamental truths apply at different levels of reality.

The eighth lesson explores the significance of the syllable "Om," describing it as a representation of Brahman and the entire universe. It outlines the diverse uses of Om in rituals, meditation, and recitation, emphasizing its central role in Vedic practices.

The ninth lesson lists the ethical duties of human beings, focusing on self-study (Svadhyaya) and the exposition of Vedic knowledge (Pravacana). It stresses the importance of living a life guided by truth, justice, austerity, and compassion, encouraging individuals to practice these virtues in their daily lives.

The tenth lesson, though obscure, seems to affirm the individual's

Self as a capable and empowered being. It uses metaphors to describe the realization of Atman-Brahman, suggesting that knowledge and self-realization can transcend the empirical world.

The eleventh lesson provides a convocation address to graduating students, outlining the ethical way of life they should follow. It advises them to take care of their health, pursue prosperity, and adhere to their responsibilities, emphasizing the importance of truthfulness, charity, and respectful conduct towards parents, teachers, and guests.

The final lesson mirrors the first, with acknowledgments and benedictions that reaffirm the teachings and promises made. It concludes with a prayer for peace, reiterating the interconnectedness of the student, teacher, and the ultimate reality.

Ananda Valli

The Ananda Valli, part of the Taittiriya Upanishad, delves into understanding the Self (Atman) and its profound connection to the ultimate reality (Brahman). This chapter teaches that realizing one's true self is the highest knowledge, leading to a state of bliss and freedom from all fears and concerns. It introduces the concept of the "Kosha" theory, which explains the layers of human existence and knowledge, gradually revealing the deepest truths about oneself.

Before diving into the teachings, the Ananda Valli begins with a prayer for protection, knowledge, and harmony between the teacher and the student. This invocation emphasizes a harmonious and peaceful relationship between the teacher and the student, setting a positive tone for the pursuit of knowledge.

The Concept of Koshas

The Ananda Valli introduces the idea of Koshas, or layers, that envelop the true self. These layers represent different aspects of human existence and knowledge, from the most superficial to the deepest. Understanding and peeling back these layers is essential for realizing one's true nature.

The Five Koshas

Annamaya Kosha (The Food Sheath):

This is the outermost layer, associated with the physical body and material existence. It includes everything related to the physical nourishment and growth of the body. The Upanishad explains that the physical body and the material world are manifestations of Brahman but are the most superficial aspects of existence. Understanding this layer involves recognizing the interdependence of all life forms and the role of food in sustaining life.

Pranamaya Kosha (The Vital Breath Sheath):

This layer represents the life-force or vital energy that animates the body. It is associated with breathing and the processes that sustain life. The life-force is more than just the physical body; it includes the vital energies that drive all living beings. Recognizing this layer involves understanding the importance of breath and life-energy in sustaining existence.

Manomaya Kosha (The Mental Sheath):

This layer pertains to the mind, thoughts, and emotions. It

includes the power of will, the ability to wish, and the striving for prosperity through actions. While the mind plays a crucial role in understanding the world, it is still an incomplete layer of knowledge. True liberation and contentment come from realizing deeper truths beyond the mind.

Vijnanamaya Kosha (The Knowledge Sheath):

This sheath represents wisdom, reason, and ethics. It is the realm of intellectual understanding and insight. Individuals aware of this layer exhibit qualities such as faith, justice, truth, and the ability to perceive deeper truths. However, even this profound knowledge is not the ultimate truth. It serves as a guide towards deeper spiritual realization.

Anandamaya Kosha (The Bliss Sheath):

This is the innermost layer, representing pure bliss and contentment. It is associated with the state of being that is in harmony with the Self and the ultimate reality, Brahman. Those who realize this layer experience love, joy, cheerfulness, and a sense of oneness with all existence. This deepest layer signifies the ultimate goal of self-knowledge, where one transcends the limitations of the material and mental realms and experiences unity with the cosmos.

The Ananda Valli teaches that true self-knowledge cannot be attained through mere ritualistic worship or by fulfilling egoistic desires. Instead, it requires deep introspection and the shedding of superficial layers of knowledge. The journey involves moving from the outermost physical layer to the innermost spiritual layer, gradually uncovering the true nature of the Self.

The culmination of understanding these layers is the realization of one's true nature as Atman, which is identical with Brahman. This realization brings about a state of liberation, characterized by the absence of fear, desire, and suffering. It is a state of profound peace, joy, and contentment, where one experiences oneness with all of reality.

The Ananda Valli provides a comprehensive framework for understanding human existence and the path to spiritual enlightenment. By exploring and transcending the layers of the Koshas, one can achieve the highest state of bliss and unity with the ultimate reality. This ancient wisdom continues to offer valuable insights into the nature of self-knowledge and the pursuit of a fulfilled life.

Bhrigu Valli

Bhrigu Valli, a key chapter in the Taittiriya Upanishad, delves into profound philosophical concepts concerning the nature of the Self (Atman) and its relationship with the ultimate reality (Brahman). This chapter not only expounds on the nature of existence but also presents these ideas through the narrative of Sage Bhrigu's spiritual quest. Bhrigu Valli is both a philosophical discourse and a practical guide, offering deep insights into the nature of reality and the path to self-realization.

The Journey of Sage Bhrigu

The narrative of Bhrigu Valli centers around Sage Bhrigu, who undertakes a quest to understand the nature of Brahman. His journey is initiated by his father, Sage Varuni, who imparts fundamental insights into the nature of Brahman. Varuni's guidance is crucial as it establishes the framework for Bhrigu's exploration. Varuni explains that Brahman is the source of all creation, the sustainer of life, and the ultimate destination where all beings return after death. This description encapsulates Brahman's all-encompassing nature and eternal essence.

Bhrigu's quest involves a process of introspection, where he examines various layers of reality to uncover the innermost truth. This journey reflects the Upanishadic method of peeling away layers of ignorance to reveal the true nature of the Self. Bhrigu's exploration is a metaphor for the spiritual path of self-discovery and enlightenment.

The Nature of Brahman

Central to Bhrigu Valli is the concept of Brahman as the ultimate reality. Brahman is described as the fundamental essence from which all beings emerge, in which they exist, and into which they ultimately dissolve. This understanding underscores the omnipresence and omnipotence of Brahman. It is the substratum of all existence, transcending the material and the temporal.

The chapter emphasizes that Brahman is not merely an abstract concept but a living reality that manifests through all forms of life. This realization is crucial for attaining self-knowledge and liberation. By recognizing Brahman's presence in all aspects of existence, one can transcend the illusions of the material world and attain a state of unity and bliss.

Food as a Metaphor for Interconnectedness

A distinctive feature of Bhrigu Valli is its use of the metaphor of "food" to explain the interconnectedness of all things. The concept of food in this context is not limited to physical nourishment but extends to energy, material substance, and knowledge. This metaphor illustrates how all elements of the universe are interrelated and dependent on one another.

The text explains that food is foundational to existence. It sustains life and facilitates the process of growth and development. Everything in the universe is part of a larger food chain, where each element provides sustenance for another. This interconnectedness highlights the unity of all things and the cyclical nature of existence.

By understanding this interconnectedness, one gains insight into the nature of reality and the essence of Brahman. The metaphor of food serves as a practical illustration of how all aspects of life are interwoven and how they contribute to the overall harmony of the universe.

The Relationship Between Bliss and Brahman

The chapter further explores the relationship between Brahman and bliss. It asserts that Brahman is the ultimate source of bliss and that all beings are born from, live through, and ultimately return to this state of bliss. This concept emphasizes that the true nature of Brahman is not just a philosophical idea but a state of profound joy and contentment.

The idea that Brahman is bliss implies that the essence of reality is inherently joyful and fulfilling. This realization shifts the focus from the pursuit of temporary pleasures to the recognition of a deeper, enduring happiness that is intrinsic to the nature of existence. By aligning oneself with this understanding, one can attain a state of inner peace and fulfillment.

The Declaration of Oneness

The concluding section of Bhrigu Valli presents a powerful declaration of oneness with the universe. It asserts that the sage who understands the nature of Brahman realizes their fundamental unity with all things. This declaration emphasizes the idea of being one with the cosmos and aligning with the universal order.

The declaration reflects the ultimate realization of the Self, where one transcends individual identity and experiences a state of complete unity and harmony with the universe. This realization leads to a profound sense of freedom and liberation, characterized by an unwavering sense of peace and joy.

Bhrigu Valli offers a profound exploration of the nature of the Self and its relationship with the ultimate reality. Through the narrative of Sage Bhrigu and the use of metaphors such as food, the chapter provides deep insights into the interconnectedness of all things and the nature of bliss. The teachings of Bhrigu Valli encourage a journey of introspection and self-discovery, leading to a realization of the true essence of Brahman and the attainment of inner peace and fulfillment. By integrating these insights into daily life, one can move towards a state of self-realization and liberation, aligning with the profound truths of the universe.

The Sound of Enlightenment

The **Hamsa Upanishad** is a minor text within Hinduism, classified as one of the twenty Yoga Upanishads and associated with the Shukla Yajurveda. It is thought to have been composed sometime between the 2nd millennium CE and the early 17th century, as it was included in the Persian translation of the Upanishads by Dara Shikoh. The text is structured as a dialogue between the sage Gautama and the divine Sanatkumara, exploring Hamsa-vidya as a prelude to Brahmavidya. It delves into the sound of Om, its connection to Hamsa, and how meditation on this sound can lead to the realization of Paramahamsa, the highest state of the soul.

Symbolism and Meaning of Hamsa

In Indian tradition, the term "Hamsa" can refer to migratory birds such as geese, swans, or flamingos. Symbolically, Hamsa represents the migrating or reincarnating soul, and by extension, the Atman (soul) and moksha (liberation). The title "Hamsa" reflects the text's focus on the journey of the individual soul towards the highest state of Paramahamsa.

The Dialogue

The Upanishad begins with the sage Gautama asking the divine Sanatkumara to distill the essence of all Vedic knowledge for him. Sanatkumara responds by recounting how Shiva pondered over the Vedas and shared this knowledge with Parvati. This wisdom, known as the path of the Hamsa, is intended for Yoga students who are self-restrained, free from worldly cravings, and devoted to learning from a Guru. Sanatkumara emphasizes that this knowledge is meant for those who have disciplined their minds and bodies, who have renounced the pursuit of worldly pleasures, and who are sincerely dedicated to their spiritual journey. This sets the stage for the exploration of Hamsa-vidya.

The Arrival of Hamsa

The text describes breath as a fundamental sound that stays within human bodies throughout their lives, providing them with energy. This breath, or Hamsa, enters at birth and dwells deeply within, akin to how fire resides invisibly within wood or oil within sesame seeds. Recognizing this Hamsa within oneself is seen as a means to attain liberation from the cycle of birth and death.

The Upanishad poetically describes the presence of Hamsa as follows:

- At birth, the breath enters the body, likened to a migratory bird entering its new abode.

- It dwells within, much like fire hidden within wood or oil within seeds.
- To realize this inner Hamsa is to free oneself from the cycle of death and rebirth.

Here, Hamsa symbolizes the Atman, or soul, that migrates through different bodies over lifetimes. Understanding and connecting with this inner Hamsa is crucial for spiritual liberation.

The Chakras

Chapter 3 of the Hamsa Upanishad describes a tantric process to energize the chakras, the energy centers within the body. The process involves:

- Pressing the heels at the anal opening to focus energy.
- Raising the breath from the Muladhara chakra (located at the base of the spine) to the Svadhisthana chakra (near the genital organs), and circumambulating there three times.
- Continuing to raise the breath to the Manipura chakra (at the navel), the Anahata chakra (at the heart), the Vishuddhi chakra (at the throat), and finally to the Ajna chakra (between the eyebrows).
- Contemplating on the Brahmarandhra (the crown chakra at the top of the head).

This meditation on Om and the chakras is aimed at realizing Brahman, the highest Atman. The process emphasizes the connection between breath, the chakras, and the divine, guiding the yogi towards spiritual enlightenment.

Hamsa as an Aphorism

The Hamsa Upanishad explains Hamsa as part of the aphorism

"Hamso Hamsa," where Hamsa represents the soul. The sound "Ham" is considered its bija (seed), and the text describes this repetition:

- A yogi experiences 21,606 Hamsas in a full day-night cycle (with each inbreathing and outbreathing counted separately).
- This constant repetition of Hamsa serves as a reminder of the soul's presence and its connection to the divine.

The Upanishad also outlines six mantra aphorisms, each starting with Om and relating to Hamsa. These mantras are tools for meditation, helping the yogi to focus on the divine sound of Om and its significance.

Hamsa in the Heart

The Upanishad instructs practitioners to meditate on Hamsa within the heart's eight-petaled lotus. Visualized with elements like Agni (fire) and Soma (nectar) as wings, and Om as the head and neck, this Hamsa is the Paramahamsa, the highest soul, pervading the universe and shining like ten million suns.

Each petal of the lotus symbolizes different aspects of life and actions:

- The east-facing petal represents noble actions.
- The southeast petal denotes sleep and indolence.
- The southwest petal indicates evil actions.
- The west-facing petal symbolizes play.
- The northwest petal relates to walking and other activities.
- The north-facing petal represents enjoying love and lust.
- The northeast petal signifies ambition and the desire to amass wealth.

The center of the lotus represents renunciation, the stamen signifies the wakeful state, the pericarp (outer layer) denotes the dreaming state, the bija (seed) symbolizes dreamless sleep, and leaving the lotus is akin to the Turya state, the experience of pure consciousness.

Hamsa and the Turya State

The Turya state, or the fourth state of pure consciousness, is achieved when Hamsa merges with the reverberation of Om. This state is not reached through the mind but through the will of the Hamsa, the soul. It signifies the ultimate unity of the individual soul with the divine.

Hamsa and Music

The Upanishad describes ten stages of "inner nada" (sounds) that a yogi experiences during meditation. These sounds progress from subtle to profound:

1. Chini (a faint sound)
2. Chini-chini (a fainter version of the first sound)
3. A bell
4. A conch shell
5. A string instrument (tantiri)
6. Clapping
7. A flute
8. A drum (bheri)
9. A kettle drum (mridangam)
10. Thunder (sound of lightning)

The Upanishad advises avoiding the first nine sounds and seeking the tenth, as it relates to Hamsa. In this tenth state, the yogi realizes

Brahman, achieving unity with the divine, where all duality vanishes. The yogi then shines with enlightenment, free from doubts and desires, experiencing calmness and bliss.

The Hamsa Upanishad offers profound insights into the nature of the soul, the process of meditation, and the path to spiritual enlightenment. Through the dialogue between Gautama and Sanatkumara, the text explores the deep connections between breath, sound, and the divine journey of the soul towards ultimate liberation. The meditation on Hamsa and the inner nada, the energizing of the chakras, and the symbolic use of the lotus all serve as powerful tools for achieving the highest state of spiritual realization, Paramahamsa.

Four Seats of Consciousness

The **Brahma Upanishad**, also known as Brahmopanishad, is a lesser-known yet profoundly significant text within Hinduism. It is categorized among the 32 Upanishads linked to the Krishna Yajurveda and is one of the 19 Sannyasa Upanishads. Composed in ancient Sanskrit, this text delves deeply into the traditions of Hindu renunciation, focusing on the Atman (soul), its various states of consciousness, and the spiritual path to realizing the Nirguna Brahman, the formless and ultimate reality.

Structure and Content

The Brahma Upanishad is structured as a dialog between the sage Pippalada and Shaunaka Mahashala, a wealthy householder seeking spiritual knowledge. The text opens with Shaunaka addressing Pippalada, referring to the human body as the "divine city of Brahman," and inquiring about the nature and source of the power within it. This sets the stage for Pippalada to impart the supreme wisdom of Brahman, illustrating the profound interconnectedness between the Atman (soul) and Brahman (the universal self).

The Nature of Brahman

In his teachings, Pippalada elucidates that Brahman is both the Prana (life-force) and the Atman (soul) within every human being. Brahman is described as the self-effulgent, controlling force that imbues the body with life and governs all its functions. This concept signifies that Brahman is not just a cosmic entity but an intimate presence within each individual, manifesting as the breath and life-force that sustain all living beings.

Four Seats and States of Consciousness

The Upanishad identifies four crucial seats within the human body where Brahman manifests:

1. **The Navel (Wakeful State)**: In this state, Brahman is equated with Brahma, the creator deity, symbolizing the active, waking consciousness.
2. **The Heart (Dream State)**: Here, Brahman is associated with Vishnu, the preserver, representing the consciousness experienced in dreams.
3. **The Throat (Dreamless Sleep State)**: In this state, Brahman is linked to Rudra, the destroyer, signifying the deep, dreamless sleep where individual consciousness is at rest.
4. **The Head (Transcendental State)**: This state embodies the Supreme Indestructible One, representing the highest state of consciousness, transcending the other three states and connecting directly with the ultimate reality.

5. These states and seats highlight the journey of consciousness from the physical waking state to the profound transcendental experience, underscoring the holistic nature of Brahman within the human experience.

Rejection of Rituals

A significant portion of the Brahma Upanishad, particularly in its third chapter, is dedicated to rejecting external rituals and religious observances. Instead, it emphasizes that the highest state of human existence is one entirely devoted to knowledge and inner realization. This aligns with the broader Upanishadic tradition that values personal spiritual insight and inner transformation over ritualistic practices.

The Sacred Thread: Symbolism and Significance

The Upanishad introduces the concept of the sacred thread (sutra), which traditionally signifies religious and spiritual purity in Hindu culture. However, the text reinterprets this thread as a symbol of the knowledge and awareness of Brahman, transcending physical rituals. It posits that the true sacred thread is the understanding and realization of Brahman itself. This symbolic reinterpretation elevates the importance of inner spiritual knowledge over external symbols, marking a profound shift in the understanding of spiritual purity and enlightenment.

The Heart as the Seat of the Universe

In a vivid and poetic description, the Brahma Upanishad portrays the heart as resembling the calyx of a lotus, full of cavities and facing downward. This imagery symbolizes the heart as the central seat of consciousness and the dwelling place of the Supreme Self. It is within this "lotus heart" that the entire universe resides, signifying the inner space where the individual self merges with the cosmic self. This metaphor highlights the profound significance of the heart as the center of spiritual realization and unity with Brahman.

Meditation and Spiritual Realization

The text guides practitioners towards a state of meditation that transcends physical exertions and external rituals. It emphasizes the unifying principle of all creatures and the importance of inner contemplation and spiritual discipline. By meditating on the self and recognizing the underlying unity of all beings, one can achieve transcendental bliss and ultimate liberation. The Upanishad underscores that true spiritual practice involves a deep inner journey, leading to the realization of the self as one with Brahman.

The Brahma Upanishad offers profound insights into the nature of the self, the journey of consciousness, and the ultimate unity with the formless Brahman. Through its teachings, it emphasizes the importance of inner knowledge, meditation, and the renunciation of external rituals. By understanding and meditating on the self within the "divine city" of the body, practitioners are guided towards achieving the highest state of spiritual enlightenment, where the individual self merges with the universal Brahman. This ancient text thus remains a timeless guide for those seeking to understand the deeper aspects of their existence and the nature of ultimate reality.

The Kaivalya

The **Kaivalya Upanishad**, a minor yet profound text within Hinduism, holds significant philosophical and spiritual insights. As a Shaiva Upanishad, it is preserved in two versions: one linked to the Krishna Yajurveda and the other to the Atharvaveda. The text is revered for integrating Shaivism within the Vedanta tradition, emphasizing the realization of Atman (self), Brahman (universal self), and the pursuit of Self-knowledge as the path to Kaivalya (liberation).

"Kaivalya" derives from the Sanskrit root "Kevala," meaning "aloneness" or "isolation." In the Upanishadic context, Kaivalya signifies a state of complete detachment from worldly desires and attachments, leading to spiritual liberation and the realization of the self's unity with Brahman. The Upanishad underscores renunciation and inner contemplation as means to achieve this state of absoluteness and inner conviction.

Structure and Themes

The Upanishad is structured as a dialog between the sage Ashvalayana and the Lord Paramesthi (Brahma). Through this discourse, the text addresses key themes such as the nature of Brahman, the importance of faith and meditation, the process of renunciation, and the ultimate goal of spiritual liberation.

The Inquiry and Response

Ashvalayana approaches Brahma, seeking the highest knowledge of Brahman. Brahma responds by emphasizing that this knowledge is attained not through work, progeny, or wealth, but through faith, devotion, meditation, and renunciation. This initial exchange sets the tone for the profound teachings that follow, highlighting the necessity of inner spiritual practices over external achievements.

Inner State and Meditation

The text provides detailed instructions on the ideal conditions for meditation:

1. **Secluded Place and Easy Posture**: The seeker is advised to meditate in a secluded place, ensuring minimal distractions. An easy, stable posture aids in maintaining physical comfort and mental focus.

2. **Purity and Control**: The importance of purity (both physical and mental) and control over the senses is stressed. Purity fosters a conducive environment for spiritual practices, while

sense control prevents distractions.

3. **Reverence to the Preceptor**: Saluting one's preceptor with reverence signifies the respect for the teacher's role in guiding the seeker. This respect and humility are crucial for receiving and internalizing spiritual teachings.

4. **Meditation on Brahman**: The seeker is instructed to meditate within the lotus of the heart on the unthinkable, formless, and eternal Brahman. This focus on the heart symbolizes turning inward to discover the true self.

Nature of the Self

The Upanishad delves into the true nature of the Self, describing it as unmanifest, endless, all-pervading consciousness, and bliss. It is depicted as the source and witness of all, transcending all dualities and attributes. Key points include:

1. **Formlessness and Eternity**: Brahman is described as formless, unmanifest, and eternal, emphasizing its transcendence beyond physical attributes and limitations.

2. **Source of All**: Brahman is the origin and sustainer of the universe, highlighting its omnipresence and omnipotence. This realization fosters a sense of unity with all existence.

3. **Witness Consciousness**: The concept of Brahman as the witness underscores the idea that the self observes all phenomena without being affected by them. This detachment is crucial for achieving liberation.

Unity with the Supreme

The Upanishad teaches that by meditating on the highest Lord, associated with Uma (Shiva's consort), the seeker realizes the unity of the Self with all divine manifestations. This realization includes:

1. **Divine Unity**: Understanding that Brahma, Shiva, Vishnu, Prana (vitality), time, and all cosmic elements are expressions of the same ultimate reality. This non-dual perspective dissolves the illusion of separateness.

2. **Transcendence**: Seeing the Atman in all beings and all beings in the Atman leads to the highest realization of Brahman. This unity and realization are achieved through the "friction of knowledge," symbolized by the sacred fire ritual, where knowledge burns away the bonds of ignorance and Maya (illusion).

States of Consciousness

The Upanishad discusses the Jiva (individual soul) and its experiences across different states of consciousness:

1. **Waking State**: In the waking state, the Jiva identifies with the body and engages in worldly activities. The experiences in this state are driven by sensory perceptions and desires.

2. **Dream State**: During the dream state, the Jiva experiences a reality created by its own mind, reflecting its desires, fears, and unresolved experiences from the waking state.

3. **Deep Sleep**: In the state of deep sleep, the Jiva exists in a state of bliss, free from the distractions of sensory inputs and mental constructs. This state symbolizes the underlying peace and contentment of the self.

4. **Return to Waking and Dream States**: The text explains how the Jiva, influenced by past actions and karma, returns to the

waking and dream states, perpetuating the cycle of birth and rebirth. True liberation involves recognizing the self as distinct from these transient states and experiences.

The Cosmic and Individual Self

The Upanishad emphasizes the non-dual nature of reality, where the individual self (Atman) is the same as the universal self (Brahman). Key teachings include:

1. **Non-Duality**: The realization that the Atman and Brahman are one and the same. This understanding dissolves the illusion of individuality and separateness, leading to a profound sense of unity and interconnectedness.

2. **Support and Dissolution**: The text teaches that all phenomena arise from, rest in, and dissolve into Brahman. This cyclical process underscores the transient nature of worldly experiences and the eternal nature of the self.

3. **Transcendence of Dualities**: By recognizing the self as the witness consciousness, distinct from the enjoyable, the enjoyer, and the enjoyment, the seeker transcends the dualities of life. This transcendence leads to liberation from the cycle of birth and rebirth.

Final Liberation

The Kaivalya Upanishad concludes by stating that those who study and internalize its teachings achieve purification from all sins and attain the knowledge that leads to liberation. The ultimate goal is to realize one's unity with the formless, eternal Paramatman, transcending all dualities and limitations. Key points include:

1. **Purification and Liberation**: The text asserts that studying

the Shatarudriya (a hymn dedicated to Rudra, a form of Shiva) and internalizing its teachings purifies the seeker from sins and leads to liberation.

2. **Eternal Peace**: The realization of the self's unity with Brahman brings about a state of eternal peace and contentment, free from the sufferings of worldly existence.

3. **Attainment of Kaivalya**: The ultimate fruit of this knowledge is Kaivalya, a state of absolute detachment and spiritual liberation, where the seeker attains oneness with the supreme reality.

The Kaivalya Upanishad presents a comprehensive guide to achieving spiritual liberation through renunciation, meditation, and the realization of the non-dual nature of the self and the universe. By emphasizing the importance of inner knowledge and detachment from worldly desires, it offers profound insights into the path of Self-realization and the attainment of Kaivalya. This ancient text remains a timeless source of wisdom for seekers of spiritual truth and enlightenment within the broader framework of Vedanta and Hindu philosophy.

I Have Renounced

The **Aruneya Upanishad** is a minor text in the collection of 108 Upanishads, associated with the Samaveda. This Upanishad is classified as a Sannyasa Upanishad, which means it focuses on the practice of Sannyasa, or renunciation. The text provides detailed instructions on the life and behavior of a Sannyasi (a Hindu monk) and outlines the characteristics of the Paramahamsa, a highly enlightened renunciant. The Upanishad is presented as a dialogue between the sage Aruni and Prajapati, a Vedic god often identified with Brahma.

The Path of Renunciation

The Upanishad begins with Aruni approaching Prajapati and asking how he can give up all rituals and external symbols of spirituality. Prajapati advises Aruni to let go of all worldly connections, including relationships with family and friends. He should also abandon physical symbols of spirituality such as the hair tuft and the sacred thread. Additionally, Prajapati instructs Aruni to give up Vedic rituals and mantras, and instead, to wear simple clothes and carry a staff, symbolizing his entry into a life of renunciation.

Prajapati goes further, instructing Aruni to detach himself from the seven upper realms (Bhur, Bhuvah, Svar, Mahas, Jana, Tapas, and Satya) and the seven lower realms (Atala, Patala, Vitala, Sutala, Rasatala, Mahatala, and Talatala). This comprehensive renunciation represents a complete detachment from the material world and all cosmic orders.

Stages of Life and Renunciation Practices

The Upanishad explains that during the three stages of life—Brahmacharya (student), Grihastha (householder), and Vanaprastha (forest dweller)—one should perform specific rituals and sacrifices. These include the Prana-Agnihotra fire sacrifices and the recitation of the Gayatri mantra. However, as a renunciant, Aruni is instructed to stop these practices and focus solely on meditation and realization of the Atman (the self). He should discard his sacred thread and engage only in the recitation of essential texts like the Aranyakas and Upanishads.

The Ritual of Renunciation

To formally embrace renunciation, Aruni should declare his departure from worldly life by repeating the phrase "I have renounced" three times. He should then pick up a bamboo staff and wear minimal clothing, symbolizing his new role as a Sannyasi. He is advised to approach food with the same detachment as if it were medicine, eating sparingly and focusing on his spiritual goals.

The Upanishad emphasizes that a renunciant must adhere to moral and ethical standards. He should practice non-violence, truthfulness, and chastity, while avoiding negative traits such as anger, greed, and deceit. The staff he carries represents support and strength, and he should view it as a friend and protector in his spiritual journey.

The Ideal Paramahamsa

The Upanishad also describes the Paramahamsa Parivrajaka, the highest level of renunciant. These wandering monks are believed to have attained the highest state of enlightenment. They live in extreme simplicity, depending entirely on alms for sustenance and avoiding all material possessions. During the rainy season, they stay in one place, but for the rest of the year, they wander alone or with a single companion.

The text highlights that a true Paramahamsa abandons all traditional symbols and materials, including the sacred thread and staff made from specific types of wood. For these enlightened sages, the mantra "Om" becomes the essence of their spiritual practice, and understanding the true meaning of the Vedas leads to liberation.

The Aruneya Upanishad provides a comprehensive guide on the practice of renunciation in Hindu philosophy. It details how to relinquish material possessions, worldly relationships, and ritualistic practices to achieve spiritual liberation. By embodying virtues such as non-violence, truthfulness, and detachment, a renunciant aims to realize the Atman and attain enlightenment. The teachings of Prajapati to Aruni offer valuable insights into the path of Sannyasa and the life of a Paramahamsa, providing a roadmap for those seeking to live a life of spiritual devotion and self-realization.

The Universe is A Creation Of Both

The **Mantrika Upanishad**, a significant yet minor text within Hindu philosophy, offers a profound synthesis of various philosophical ideas. Originating from the Shukla Yajurveda, it belongs to the Vedanta and Yoga traditions and is listed as the 32nd in the Muktika canon of 108 Upanishads. Comprising 21 verses, this Upanishad blends concepts from Samkhya, Yoga, Vedanta, and Bhakti, presenting a theistic view of Yoga.

Its exploration of the relationship between Brahman and Maya sets the stage for a deeper understanding of the nature of existence. Brahman, the changeless reality, and Maya, the illusory reality, are central to the Upanishad's teachings. It posits that Brahman resides within the body as the soul, undergoing countless transformations, illustrating the interplay between the infinite and the finite, the eternal and the transient. This foundational concept underscores the transient nature of physical existence and the eternal aspect of the soul, aligning with the broader Vedantic view of the self.

Core Concepts

At the core of the Mantrika Upanishad is the theory of creation involving Purusha and Prakriti. The text suggests that the universe is a creation of both Purusha (the cosmic spirit) and Prakriti (the material nature). These two fundamental entities collaborate in the process of creation, where various souls, described as infants, partake in this divine play by drawing sustenance from the inactive Ishvara (God), treating this interaction as a Vedic sacrifice. This syncretic approach highlights the interdependent relationship between the cosmic spirit and material nature, presenting a unified vision of creation that resonates with theistic interpretations of Yoga and Vedanta. The Upanishad emphasizes the importance of understanding this dynamic interplay to grasp the nature of the universe and the soul's role within it.

The role of Maya is elaborately discussed in the Mantrika Upanishad, portraying it as the creative force with both a beginning and an end, fulfilling all desires and encompassing all experiences. Maya is depicted as the Lord's mighty power, through which beings are brought into existence, characterized by the colors white, black, and red. The Lord enjoys and sustains Maya, highlighting a dynamic and reciprocal relationship between the divine and the material world. This portrayal of Maya emphasizes its role in the process of creation and sustenance, illustrating the complexities of the material world and its relationship with the divine. The Upanishad's detailed description of Maya's functions and attributes provides a deeper understanding of its significance in Hindu cosmology.

The perception of the Absolute is another crucial theme in the Mantrika Upanishad. It posits that sages established in Sattva (purity and goodness) can perceive the Absolute beyond the three Gunas (qualities of nature: Sattva, Rajas, Tamas). This perception is achieved by dissolving ignorance through the light of knowledge, leading to the realization of the Absolute's true nature. The Upanishad emphasizes that this knowledge is not easily accessible and requires a profound inner transformation. This theme aligns with the broader goals of Vedantic and Yogic practices, which aim to transcend the limitations of the material world and realize the ultimate truth. The Upanishad acknowledges various philosophical systems like Sankhya, which enumerates principles of existence. It mentions the classification of elements and the different views on the nature of the Supreme Principle, whether non-dual, dual, or manifold. This inclusive approach reflects the richness and diversity of Hindu philosophical thought, recognizing the validity of multiple perspectives on the nature of reality. By incorporating these different viewpoints, the Mantrika Upanishad offers a comprehensive framework for understanding the complexities of existence and the divine. This recognition of diverse philosophical systems underscores the text's syncretic nature and its attempt to harmonize various schools of thought within Hinduism.

Unity of all existence is a recurring theme in the Mantrika Upanishad. It emphasizes that the diverse manifestations of the universe are ultimately woven into and dissolved back into Brahman, the infinite reality. This cyclical process underscores the impermanence of the material world and the eternal nature of the divine. The Upanishad describes how all manifestations merge back into Brahman, highlighting the fundamental unity underlying all existence. This theme resonates with the Vedantic view of the oneness of all reality, emphasizing the interconnectedness of the universe and the ultimate goal of realizing this unity. The Upanishad's exploration of this theme provides a profound understanding of the nature of existence and the path to liberation.

Knowledge and liberation are central to the teachings of the Mantrika Upanishad. It posits that the ultimate goal is the realization of Brahman, where those who attain this knowledge merge into the infinite, transcending the cycle of birth and death. This dissolution into the infinite is seen as the final liberation, highlighting the transformative power of knowledge and the importance of inner realization. The Upanishad emphasizes the significance of attaining this knowledge to achieve liberation, aligning with the broader goals of Vedantic and Yogic practices. This focus on knowledge and liberation underscores the text's emphasis on the transformative potential of spiritual practices and the importance of realizing the ultimate truth.

In conclusion, the **Mantrika Upanishad** provides a rich tapestry of philosophical ideas, blending concepts from different traditions to present a holistic view of existence. It emphasizes the interplay between the infinite and the finite, the eternal and the transient, and the dynamic relationship between the divine and the material world. Through its exploration of these themes, the Upanishad offers profound insights into the nature of reality and the path to liberation. Its synthesis of various philosophical systems and its emphasis on the unity of all existence highlight its significance within Hindu philosophical thought, providing a comprehensive framework for understanding the complexities of existence and the divine.

The Ideal Renunciant

The **Jabala Upanishad** is a seminal text within the corpus of Hindu philosophical literature, particularly among the Sannyasa Upanishads. Attached to the Shukla Yajurveda, this Upanishad dates back to around the 3rd century BCE and stands as one of the earliest works exploring the themes of renunciation (Sannyasa) and spiritual realization. Its teachings emphasize the profound inner journey towards understanding the Self (Atman) and the ultimate reality (Brahman), advocating for a departure from worldly attachments to achieve spiritual enlightenment.

The Concept of Avimukta

The Jabala Upanishad introduces the concept of "Avimukta" as a central theme in its spiritual discourse. Avimukta is described as the highest sacred space, equated with the renowned holy site of Kurukshetra. However, the Upanishad offers a more esoteric interpretation: Avimukta represents an inner spiritual space located between the eyebrows, symbolizing the divine essence within every individual. This sacred inner realm is depicted as the point where vital energies (prana) leave the body, marking the transition to liberation (moksha). The text instructs that one should constantly perceive this inner space as the sacred Kurukshetra, thereby internalizing the divine presence rather than relying solely on external pilgrimage sites.

The Practice of Renunciation

The Jabala Upanishad presents a flexible approach to renunciation, which is not confined to any specific life stage but is seen as a personal choice. It emphasizes that renunciation can be embraced by individuals at various stages of life, whether they are students (Brahmacharins), householders (Grihasthas), or forest-dwellers (Vanaprasthas). The text acknowledges that one can even choose to renounce worldly life from a young age or at any point when a deep disillusionment with material existence arises. This approach underlines the Upanishad's recognition of individual spiritual readiness over rigid adherence to traditional life stages.

The concept of mental renunciation is also highlighted, where individuals who are physically incapacitated can still achieve a state of detachment through mental resolve. This inclusive view reflects the text's emphasis on the inner dimension of spiritual practice rather than just the external performance of rituals.

Spiritual Practices and Ethics

Central to the Jabala Upanishad is the practice of meditation on Avimukta. This practice involves focusing on the inner space between the eyebrows, which is seen as the seat of divine consciousness. The text posits that such meditation leads to the realization of the infinite and unmanifest Self, which is essential for spiritual liberation. The Upanishad places greater importance on this internal worship over external rituals, which are seen as secondary to the direct experience of the divine within oneself.

In addition to meditation, the text underscores the importance of ethical conduct for a true renunciant. A sincere practitioner must live a life of non-harm (ahimsa) in thought, word, and deed, reflecting the inner purity required for spiritual progress. This ethical living supports the overarching goal of achieving unity with Brahman and attaining liberation.

The Role of Mantras and Rituals

The Jabala Upanishad acknowledges the significance of mantras in the spiritual journey, particularly the Satarudriya mantra. This mantra, associated with Rudra (a form of Shiva), is believed to confer immortality and spiritual enlightenment. Reciting this mantra aligns the practitioner with divine forces and facilitates the path to liberation.

The text also discusses certain traditional rituals, such as the traidhataviya sacrifice, which are intended to support the practitioner's spiritual journey. However, it emphasizes that these rituals are secondary to the internal realization of Brahman. The performance of these rituals, including the offering of oblations in fire or water, serves to reinforce one's spiritual focus and commitment to the path of renunciation.

Path of the Renunciant (Sannyasa)

The Upanishad outlines various paths to renunciation, providing flexibility based on individual circumstances. It describes the stages of life through which one may progress, including the student, householder, and forest-dweller stages. Alternatively, the text acknowledges that one can take up renunciation directly from any stage of life upon realizing a deep-seated disillusionment with worldly pursuits.

The ideal renunciant, or Sannyasin, is characterized by minimal attachment to worldly possessions and symbols. The Upanishad describes such a sage as living in complete simplicity, often without any fixed abode, and accepting only what is necessary for sustenance. This lifestyle reflects a profound inner detachment and commitment to the realization of Brahman.

The Ideal Renunciant: The Paramahamsa

The concept of the Paramahamsa, or the supreme sage, is elaborated in the Jabala Upanishad. Such sages, including historical figures like Samvartaka and Dattatreya, are described as having transcended worldly attachments and dualities. They live in utter simplicity, often appearing to be beyond worldly norms, yet they embody the highest spiritual realization.

The Upanishad explains that Paramahamsas discard physical symbols of renunciation, such as the sacred thread and staff, and live in a state of pure consciousness. Their focus is entirely on the inner realization of Brahman, and their external appearance is a reflection of their deep spiritual state. These sages are described as existing in a state of equanimity and peace, embodying the ultimate goal of spiritual practice.

Realization and Peace

The Jabala Upanishad concludes with a powerful affirmation of Brahman as infinite and eternal. The realization of this truth is said to bring about liberation and a profound sense of inner peace. The text calls for a comprehensive peace that encompasses oneself, one's environment, and the forces that influence one's life. This holistic approach to peace and realization underscores the Upanishad's emphasis on inner spiritual fulfillment as the ultimate goal of human life.

By focusing on inner realization and ethical living, the Jabala Upanishad offers a profound guide for those seeking liberation. It challenges conventional views by promoting a flexible approach to renunciation and emphasizing the inner journey over external practices.

Sacred Ash of Shiva

The Brihad Jabala Upanishad is a minor but significant Hindu scripture attached to the Atharvaveda and part of the Shaiva Upanishads. It focuses on the sacred practices involving Bhasma (sacred ash) and Rudraksha (prayer beads) and is presented as a dialogue between Sage Bhusunda and Kalagni Rudra, an aspect of the god Shiva.

Understanding Sacred Ash

The first chapter begins with Sage Bhusunda asking Kalagni Rudra about the sacred ash known as Bhasma. Kalagni Rudra refers Bhusunda to the teachings of Sage Pippalada but agrees to share insights from the Brihad Jabala Upanishad. He explains that there are five types of sacred ash:

1. **Vibhoothi** - This ash comes from the face of Shiva associated with the earth element.
   with the earth element.

2. **Bhasita** - This type is linked with water and comes from another face of Shiva.

3. **Bhasma** - Connected with fire, this ash is derived from a different face of Shiva.

4. **Kshara** - Related to the wind element, this ash originates from another face of Shiva.

5. **Raksha** - This form is associated with ether and comes from yet another face of Shiva.

Each type of ash is made from a specific form of Shiva and has different uses and spiritual benefits.

The Ritual of Ash Bathing

In this chapter, Bhusunda asks about the ritual of bathing in sacred ash, known as Bhasma Snana. Kalagni Rudra explains that Bhasma represents the balance between Agni (fire) and Soma (moon), which are complementary forces. Applying Bhasma to the body involves mixing it with mantras. This practice is believed to purify the person and lead to spiritual liberation (mukti). The ritual is significant for achieving a state of purity and immortality in the context of yoga.

How to Prepare Sacred Ash

This chapter details the preparation process for making Bhasma:

1. Choosing the Cow - The dung of a brown cow mixed with cow urine is considered most effective.

2. Collection and Rituals - The dung and urine should be collected with reverence and mixed carefully.

3. Burning Process - The mixture is shaped into balls, dried, and

burned in a fire-sacrifice called Homa for three days, using corn chaff as fuel.

4. Final Preparation - On the fourth day, the resulting ash is mixed with perfumes and other substances to enhance its qualities.

Different types of Bhasma are identified:

- **Anukalpa:** Made through specific fire sacrifices.
- **Upakalpa:** Created from burning dried cow dung.
- **Upopakalpa:** Made with cow dung and urine following specific rules.
- **Akalpa:** Obtained from Shiva temples.
- Each type of Bhasma has its own method of preparation and spiritual significance.

Applying Sacred Ash and the Tripundra

The fourth chapter covers how to apply Bhasma to the body, known as Bhasma Snana, and the practice of Tripundra. There are two main types of Bhasma Snana:

1. **Malasnana:** General application of Bhasma on the whole body for purification.
2. **Vidhisnana:** Ritual application of Bhasma on specific parts of the body, such as the head, chest, and feet, with prescribed mantras.

The Tripundra, which consists of three horizontal lines of ash on the forehead, is discussed. It can be applied to various body parts, including the forehead, arms, and back. Each location has its associated deity and specific benefits, such as removing sins and enhancing spiritual progress.

Rules and Importance of Bhasma

This chapter outlines the rules for using Bhasma according to caste and life stages. It emphasizes the importance of wearing Bhasma and Tripundra regularly to avoid negative effects and to maintain spiritual purity. Bhasma is said to cleanse sins and protect against negative influences. Disregarding the Tripundra is considered an insult to Shiva, stressing its importance in daily spiritual practices.

Stories Highlighting the Power of Bhasma

Kalagni Rudra shares stories to illustrate the miraculous power of Bhasma:

- A Brahmin named Karuna was revived twice from death using Bhasma.
- The gods were saved from sin through the use of Bhasma by Sage Durvasa.
- Vishnu applied Bhasma based on Shiva's advice, demonstrating its divine significance.

These stories highlight the extraordinary power and spiritual importance of Bhasma in various contexts.

Dialogues with King Janaka and Sage Yajnavalkya

In this chapter, King Janaka and Sage Yajnavalkya discuss Tripundra and Bhasma. They seek further knowledge from Brahma, Vishnu, and Kalagni Rudra. The chapter reinforces the spiritual benefits of wearing Bhasma and Tripundra and mentions Rudraksha beads as another significant spiritual tool.

The Benefits of Studying the Brihad Jabala Upanishad

The final chapter extols the benefits of regularly studying the Brihad Jabala Upanishad. It is said that those who read this text will be purified, gain divine powers, be absolved of sins, and obtain the merit of studying other sacred scriptures. Reading the Brihad Jabala Upanishad is considered superior to other texts and leads to attaining the highest spiritual abode.

In summary, the Brihad Jabala Upanishad provides a comprehensive guide to the use and significance of sacred ash and Rudraksha beads in Shaivism. Through its teachings, it outlines rituals, preparation methods, and the profound spiritual benefits of these practices.

Twenty-Three Fundamental Questions Of Philosophy

The **Sarvasara Upanishad** stands as a profound text within Hindu philosophy, offering an extensive glossary of Vedantic terms and concepts. This Upanishad, composed in Sanskrit, is one of the 22 Samanya (general) Upanishads, which are considered pivotal in the study of Hindu metaphysics. The Sarvasara Upanishad is unique in its approach, providing a systematic exploration of key philosophical ideas through a series of questions and answers that delve into the nature of reality, consciousness, and the self.

Fundamental Concepts and Glossary

The Sarvasara Upanishad begins by presenting twenty-three fundamental questions that address core Vedantic concepts. These questions include inquiries into the nature of Moksha (liberation), Avidya (incorrect knowledge), Vidya (correct knowledge), and various states of consciousness. Each question is meticulously answered, providing a comprehensive understanding of these essential ideas. The text is structured in the style of a glossary, systematically explaining these terms to facilitate a deeper grasp of Vedantic philosophy.

Bandha (Bondage)

Bandha, or bondage, refers to the condition of being tied to the cycle of birth, death, and rebirth through attachment and egoism. According to the Sarvasara Upanishad, this bondage arises from the misidentification of the self with the body and mind, leading to a life driven by desires and aversions. Egoism, the false identification with the non-self, binds the soul to the material world and obscures its true nature. This bondage is the root cause of suffering and ignorance.

Moksha (Liberation)

Moksha is described as the liberation from the cycle of birth and death, achieved through the cessation of egoism and the realization of the true self. It is the ultimate goal of human life, signifying the attainment of eternal bliss and freedom. Liberation is attained when one transcends the limitations of the ego and recognizes the self as identical with Brahman, the ultimate reality. The Upanishad emphasizes that Moksha is not merely an escape from worldly existence but a profound realization of one's true nature.

Avidya (Incorrect Knowledge)

Avidya, or incorrect knowledge, is the ignorance that causes the misperception of reality. It is the fundamental cause of egoism and bondage, leading individuals to identify with the transient body and mind rather than the eternal self. Avidya is the veil of illusion that obscures the true nature of the self and perpetuates the cycle of samsara (birth, death, and rebirth). Overcoming Avidya through the acquisition of true knowledge is essential for liberation.

Vidya (Correct Knowledge)

Vidya is the correct knowledge that dispels Avidya and leads to the realization of the self. It is the understanding that the self (Atman) is identical with Brahman, the ultimate reality. Vidya transforms one's perception, turning the mind away from the transient and towards the eternal. This knowledge is not merely intellectual but experiential, resulting in the direct realization of the true nature of the self. Vidya is the key to liberation, as it removes the ignorance that binds the soul to the material world.

States of Consciousness

The Sarvasara Upanishad explores the various states of consciousness that the self experiences. These states include Jagrat (waking), Swapna (dream), Sushupti (deep sleep), and Turiya (the fourth state).

Jagrat (Waking Consciousness)

Jagrat, or waking consciousness, is the state in which the self perceives gross objects through the senses. In this state, the mind and senses are active, engaging with the external world. The Upanishad explains that during Jagrat, the self experiences the physical world and is influenced by the sensory inputs and the desires they generate. This state is characterized by a sense of individual identity and interaction with the material environment.

Swapna (Dream Sleep Consciousness)

Swapna, or dream sleep consciousness, is the state where the self experiences subtle objects and desires in the absence of external sensory inputs. In this state, the mind creates a reality of its own, influenced by the impressions and experiences accumulated during waking consciousness. The Upanishad highlights that Swapna is a reflection of the mind's latent desires and unresolved thoughts, manifesting as dream experiences.

Sushupti (Dreamless Deep Sleep Consciousness)

Sushupti, or dreamless deep sleep consciousness, is the state characterized by the absence of differentiated knowledge and sensory activity. In Sushupti, the mind and senses are inactive, and there is no perception of either gross or subtle objects. The Upanishad describes this state as one of profound rest and unawareness, where the self remains as a witness without any involvement in the activities of the mind or senses.

Turiya (The Fourth State)

Turiya, or the fourth state, transcends the other three states of consciousness. It is the state of pure consciousness, where the self remains as a witness to the activities of the mind and senses but is not affected by them. Turiya is described as nondual, beyond waking, dreaming, and deep sleep. It represents the realization of the self's true nature, free from all limitations and dualities. In Turiya, the self experiences oneness with Brahman, the ultimate reality.

The Five Sheaths (Koshas)

The Sarvasara Upanishad also elaborates on the five sheaths (Koshas) that encase the self, each representing different levels of existence and consciousness.

Annamaya Kosha (Food Sheath)

The **Annamaya Kosha**, or food sheath, is the outermost layer, composed of physical matter derived from food. It represents the physical body and its functions. This sheath is responsible for the body's growth, maintenance, and decay, and it is the most gross and tangible aspect of human existence.

Pranamaya Kosha (Vital Air Sheath)

The **Pranamaya Kosha**, or vital air sheath, encompasses the life force (Prana) that animates the physical body. It includes the various vital functions such as respiration, circulation, and digestion. This sheath is subtler than the Annamaya Kosha and serves as the link between the physical body and the mind.

Manomaya Kosha (Mental Sheath)

The **Manomaya Kosha**, or mental sheath, consists of the mind and emotions. It is responsible for thoughts, feelings, desires, and sensory perceptions. This sheath is subtler than the Pranamaya Kosha and plays a crucial role in shaping one's experiences and responses to the external world.

Vijnanamaya Kosha (Intellectual Sheath)

The **Vijnanamaya Kosha**, or intellectual sheath, comprises the intellect and cognitive functions. It is responsible for discrimination, decision-making, and understanding. This sheath is subtler than the

Manomaya Kosha and is associated with the ability to discern the true nature of the self.

Anandamaya Kosha (Bliss Sheath)

The **Anandamaya Kosha**, or bliss sheath, is the innermost layer, representing the experience of bliss and joy. It is the subtlest of all the sheaths and is closest to the true self. This sheath is experienced in deep meditation and the realization of the self's unity with Brahman.

The Concept of the Self

The Sarvasara Upanishad provides an in-depth exploration of the self (Atman) through various terms, each representing different aspects of the self's relationship with the body, mind, and ultimate reality.

Karta (Agent)

The **Karta**, or agent, is the self identified with the body and mind, performing actions and experiencing their results. It is the aspect of the self that is engaged in worldly activities and driven by desires and aversions.

Jiva (Individual Self)

The **Jiva**, or individual self, is the self limited by the upadhis (limiting adjuncts) of the body and mind. It is the personal, embodied soul that undergoes the cycle of birth, death, and rebirth, influenced by karma.

Kshetrajna (Knower of the Body)

The **Kshetrajna**, or knower of the body, is the self that is aware of the body's activities and experiences. It is the witness of the body's functions and the mind's movements, remaining detached and unchanging.

Saksin (Witness)

The **Saksin**, or witness, is the self that observes the manifestations and disappearances of knowledge, the knower, and the knowable. It is self-luminous and unaffected by the activities it witnesses, representing the pure awareness of the self.

Kutastha

The **Kutastha** is the self perceived in an undifferentiated manner in the intelligence of all beings. It resides in the intelligence of all beings, from Brahma (the Creator) to an ant, as the unchanging, imperishable essence.

Antaryamin (Internal Ruler)

The **Antaryamin**, or internal ruler, is the self that manifests as the inner guide, interwoven in all bodies like a thread through a string of jewels. It is the means of realizing the true nature of the self and the ultimate reality.

Pratyagatman (Inner Self)

The **Pratyagatman**, or inner self, is the self shining forth as pure consciousness, free from all limiting adjuncts. It is the essence of "Thou" (Tvam), representing the individual self in its purest form.

Paramatman (Supreme Self)

The **Paramatman**, or supreme self, is the ultimate reality, characterized by Satya (truth), Jnana (knowledge), Ananta (eternity), and Ananda (bliss). It is the nondual consciousness that transcends all limitations and distinctions, representing the essence of "That" (Tat).

The **Sarvasara Upanishad** offers a rich and detailed exposition of key Vedantic concepts, providing a comprehensive glossary of terms that are central to Hindu philosophy. Through its systematic exploration of these concepts, the text serves as a valuable resource for understanding the foundational principles of Vedanta. The Upanishad emphasizes the importance of transcending the ego, acquiring true knowledge, and realizing the self's unity with Brahman to attain liberation. This profound understanding of the self and its relationship with the ultimate reality forms the core of Vedantic philosophy, guiding seekers on the path to self-realization and eternal bliss.

What Is Atma ?

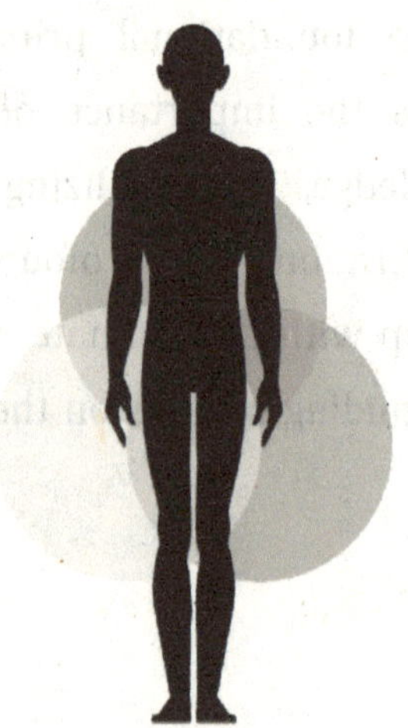

The **Atma Upanishad** is an essential but often overlooked text within the vast corpus of Hindu philosophical literature. Written in the classical Sanskrit language, this Upanishad is one of the 31 minor Upanishads associated with the Atharvaveda. Despite its classification as a minor text, the Atma Upanishad holds profound teachings about the nature of the self (Atman) and its relationship with the universal essence, Brahman. It is categorized as both a Samanya (general) and Vedantic Upanishad, emphasizing its broad applicability and deep philosophical insights.

Three Types of Self

The Atma Upanishad presents a detailed analysis of the self, dividing it into three distinct types: the Bahya-atma (external self), the Antar-atma (inner self), and the Param-atma (highest self). Each of these aspects represents a different level of existence and consciousness, leading to a comprehensive understanding of the self's true nature.

Bahya-atma (External Self)

The **Bahya-atma**, or external self, refers to the physical body. This self is composed of various anatomical parts and organs that enable sensory perception and physical actions. The text provides a detailed enumeration of these components, including the skin, flesh, hair, limbs, backbone, nails, and various bodily parts such as the stomach, navel, penis, hips, thighs, cheeks, ears, eyebrows, forehead, hands, flanks, head, and eyes. These elements constitute the physical body, which is born, grows, ages, and eventually perishes.

The external self is characterized by its material and transient nature. It engages with the world through the senses, perceiving and reacting to external stimuli. The physical body is subject to the cycle of birth and death, and its existence is marked by impermanence. This level of self is essential for experiencing the material world, but it is not the true essence of one's being.

Antar-atma (Inner Self)

The **Antar-atma**, or inner self, represents the individual soul or consciousness that resides within the physical body. This self perceives and interacts with the five elements: Prithvi (Earth), Ap (Water), Vayu (Air), Agni (Fire), and Akasha (Ether). It is the seat of mental activities, emotions, and intellect. The inner self is responsible for the functions of perception, memory, and cognition. It experiences the empirical world through consciousness and engages in various activities such as speaking, dancing, singing, and other expressions of life.

The text describes the inner self as being subject to desires, aversions, pleasure, pain, ambition, anger, fear, greed, and other psychological states. It is influenced by the mind (Manas) and consciousness (Cit), which together constitute its essence. The inner self is also capable of intellectual discrimination, distinguishing between different philosophical systems like Nyaya (logic), Mimamsa (ritual exegesis), Puranas (mythology), and various Dharmashastras (legal and ethical texts). This level of self is dynamic and multifaceted, reflecting the complexity of human consciousness and its interactions with the world.

Param-atma (Highest Self)

The **Param-atma,** or highest self, is the ultimate reality and the supreme aspect of the self. It is synonymous with Brahman, the universal soul. The Param-atma transcends the physical and mental limitations of the external and inner selves. It is described as partless, spotless, changeless, desireless, and indescribable. This highest self is pure consciousness, beyond sensory experiences, ego, and worldly attributes.

The Param-atma is eternal, uncreated, and indestructible. It is not subject to birth, death, or decay. The text emphasizes that this self cannot be divided, burnt, or destroyed. It has no limbs, no stains, no conflicts, no expectations, and is untouched by the feelings of the sensory organs or ego. The highest self is detached from the external and inner selves, existing as a pure, all-pervading, and immutable essence. It is the infinite Brahman, the Purusha, that is neither born nor dies. This self is to be realized and meditated upon through yogic practices and deep contemplation.

Manifestations of the Self

The Atma Upanishad elaborates on the manifestations of the self, explaining how the external, internal, and supreme selves interact and coexist.

External Self

The **External Self** is the physical body composed of various organs and parts, functioning through sensory perception and physical actions. It is born, grows, ages, and eventually perishes, encapsulating the material aspect of human existence. The external self engages with the world through the senses, enabling us to perceive, react, and interact with our environment.

Internal Self

The **Internal Self** perceives the five elements and engages in mental and emotional activities. It experiences the world through consciousness, marked by psychological states and intellectual discrimination. This self is subject to desires, fears, ambitions, and other mental fluctuations, reflecting the dynamic nature of the individual soul. The internal self is responsible for our mental and emotional life, influencing how we think, feel, and act.

Supreme Self

The **Supreme Self** is the ultimate, partless reality, identified with Brahman. It is beyond physical and mental attributes, existing as pure consciousness. The Supreme Self is eternal, immutable, and all-pervading, untainted by the limitations and dualities of the external and inner selves. It represents the highest truth and the ultimate goal of spiritual realization.

Yogic Practices and Meditation

To realize the highest self, the Atma Upanishad advocates practicing yoga. These practices are designed to transcend the limitations of the body and mind, leading to the direct experience of the Param-atma. The yogic practices include:

- **Breath Control (Pranayama)**: Regulating the breath to calm the mind and body, facilitating deeper concentration and meditation.

- **Sense Withdrawal (Pratyahara)**: Detaching the mind from sensory inputs, allowing one to focus inward and minimize external distractions.

- **Concentration (Dharana) and Meditation (Dhyana)**: Deep contemplation on the supreme self, transcending mental and physical distractions to achieve a state of pure awareness.

Through these practices, one can realize the highest self, experiencing its true nature as the infinite, partless, and pure Brahman. This realization is described as beyond comprehension, similar to how the seed of a ficus tree or millet cannot be fully understood even when broken into numerous parts. The Param-atma is partless and beyond properties and qualities, existing as pure, undivided consciousness.

The Pure, Non-dual Brahman

The Atma Upanishad emphasizes the non-dual nature of Brahman, stating that:

- **Brahman Alone Exists**: Beyond distinctions such as teacher and disciple, affirmation and negation, Brahman alone shines forth as the ultimate reality. It is the singular truth underlying all existence.

- **No Duality**: In the highest truth, there is neither knowledge nor ignorance, neither the world nor individual distinctions. Brahman is pure, non-dual, and ever-present. This non-dual nature means that all apparent differences and distinctions are ultimately illusory.

The Illusion of Empirical Life

The Upanishad asserts that empirical life, characterized by the perception of the world as real, is an illusion created by ignorance (Avidya). The realization of Brahman dissolves this illusion, leading to liberation (Moksha). Bondage and liberation are seen as constructs of Maya (illusion), not affecting the true self, which remains ever-free and pure.

- **Appearance of Reality**: The empirical world appears real due to ignorance, but this perception is an illusion. When one realizes the true nature of Brahman, this illusion is dispelled.
- **Liberation from Illusion**: The realization of Brahman leads to liberation, freeing one from the cycle of birth and death and the dualities of pleasure and pain, good and evil.

The **Atma Upanishad** provides a profound exploration of the nature of the self, distinguishing between the external, internal, and supreme selves. Through yogic practices and meditation, one can transcend the limitations of the body and mind, realizing the eternal, non-dual nature of Brahman. This realization leads to liberation from the cycle of birth and death, revealing the self's true, immutable essence as pure consciousness. The text emphasizes that the true self is beyond physical and mental attributes, existing as a partless, spotless, and changeless reality, embodying the ultimate truth of non-dual Brahman.

Hindu/Sanskrit Glossary

- **ABHAYAM**: Fearless.
- **ABHIMANA**: Egoism, identification with the body.
- **ABHYASA**: Spiritual practice.
- **ADHIKARI**: A qualified person.
- **ADHISHTHANA**: Substratum, support.
- **ADHYASA**: Superimposition or false attribution of properties of one thing on another thing.
- **ADHYATMIC**: Spiritual.
- **ADHYAYANA**: Study.
- **ADVAITA**: Non-duality.
- **AGRAHYA**: Unknowable.
- **AHANKARA**: Egoism.
- **AHIMSA**: Non-injury in thought, word, and deed.
- **AISVARYA**: Divine powers.
- **AJARAM**: Without old age.
- **ALABDHABHUMIKATVA**: The feeling that it is impossible to see reality.
- **ALASYA**: Laziness.
- **AMARA**: Immortal.
- **AMARA-PURUSHA**: Immortal being.
- **AMRITAM**: Immortal.
- **ANADI**: Beginningless.
- **ANAHATA**: Mystic sound heard by Yogis.
- **ANANDA**: Bliss, happiness, joy.
- **ANANDA-GHANA**: Cloud of bliss.

- **ANANDA-SVARUPA**: Of the form of bliss.
- **ANANDAMAYA**: Full of great happiness.
- **ANTAHKARANA**: Internal instrument such as mind, intellect, ego, and the subconscious mind.
- **ANANTAM**: Infinity.
- **ANTARATMAN**: Inner Self.
- **ANTARYAMIN**: Inner witness.
- **ANUBHAVA**: Experience.
- **APTA**: Realized.
- **ARHATA**: A perfected Soul.
- **ASAMPRAJNATA**: Highest super conscious state where the mind is completely annihilated and Reality experienced.
- **ASANA**: A bodily pose or posture.
- **ASHRAM**: A hermitage; monastery.
- **ASHTANGA**: Eight limbs.
- **ASURIC**: Demoniacal.
- **ATMA-JNANA**: Knowledge of the Self.
- **BENARES**: A holy pilgrimage center of Hindus, now called Varanasi in Uttar Pradesh, India.
- **BHAGAVAD-GITA**: A scripture containing Lord Krishna's teachings.
- **BHAGAVATA**: Name of a Purana (sacred work dealing with the doctrines of creation, etc.).
- **BHAJAN**: Devotional song.
- **BHAKTA**: Devotee of God.
- **BHAKTI**: Devotion.
- **BHARATAVARSHA**: India.
- **BHAVA(NA)**: Feeling; mental attitude.

- **BHAYANAKA-SABDA**: A fear-inducing sound.
- **BHOGI**: Enjoyer.
- **BHUMA**: The Unconditioned, the Great Infinite, Brahman.
- **BHUTA-SIDDHI**: A psychic power by which mastery is gained over the elements.
- **BODHISATTVA**: A being who, having developed the Awakening Mind (a mind infused with the aspiration to attain the state of Buddhahood), devotes his life to the task of achieving Buddhahood for the sake of all sentient beings.
- **BRAHMA-CHINTANA**: Constant thinking of Brahman.
- **BRAHMA-JNANA**: Direct Knowledge of Brahman.
- **BRAHMA-NISHTHA**: One who is established in the Knowledge of Brahman.
- **BRAHMA-SROTRI**: One who has knowledge of the Vedas and the Upanishads.
- **BRAHMA-SUTRAS**: Classical Vedantic scripture.
- **BRAHMA-TEJAS**: Spiritual halo.
- **BRAHMA-VIDYA**: The science of Brahman, knowledge of Brahman, learning pertaining to Brahman or the Absolute Reality.
- **BRAHMACHARYA**: Practice of celibacy. Purity in thought, word, and deed.
- **BRAHMAMUHURTA**: Period from 4 a.m. to 6 a.m.
- **BRAHMAN**: The Absolute Reality; God.
- **BRIHADARANYAKA**: Name of an Upanishad.
- **BUDDHA**: One who is totally purified from all defilements and who has realized all that can be known.
- **BUDDHI**: Intellect.

- **CHAITANYA**: Pure Consciousness.
- **CHAKRAS**: Centers of energy in the human system.
- **CHANDOGYA**: Name of an Upanishad.
- **CHELA**: Disciple.
- **CHIRANJIVI**: One who has gained eternal life.
- **CHITTA**: Subconscious mind.
- **DAIVIC**: Divine.
- **DAMA**: Control of senses.
- **DARSHAN**: Vision.
- **DAYA**: Mercy.
- **DEHA**: Body.
- **DEVAS**: Celestial beings.
- **DHARANA**: Concentration.
- **DHARMA**: Righteous way of living as enjoined by the sacred scriptures, virtue.
- **DHYANA**: Meditation.
- **DIVYA-DRISHTI**: Divine perception.
- **DVESHA**: Repulsion; hatred; dislike.
- **EKADASI**: Eleventh day of the Hindu lunar fortnight.
- **GANDHA**: Smell.
- **GUNA**: Quality born of nature.
- **GURU**: Teacher; preceptor.
- **HAVAN**: Sacred oblations.
- **HIRANYAGARBHA**: Cosmic intelligence; the supreme lord of the universe; cosmic mind.
- **INDRA**: The Lord of gods; the ruler of heaven.
- **INDRIYAS**: Senses.
- **ISHVARA**: Lord; God.

- **JADA**: Insentient.
- **JAPA**: Repetition of the Lord's Name.
- **JIVA**: Individual Soul.
- **JIVANMUKTA**: One who is liberated in this life.
- **JNANA**: Knowledge; wisdom.
- **JNANA-INDRIYAS**: Organs of knowledge or perception.
- **JNANI**: (Pronounced Nyani) A wise person.
- **KAIVALYA**: Emancipation; state of absolute independence.
- **KARMA**: Actions operating through the law of cause and effect.
- **KARMA-INDRIYAS**: Organs of action - tongue, hands, feet, genital organ, and anus.
- **KARMA-KANDI**: One who observes strictly the duties ordained in the scriptures.
- **KIRTAN**: Singing devotional songs.
- **KRIYA**: A type of exercise in Hatha Yoga.
- **KSHAMA**: Forgiveness.
- **KUNDALINI**: The primordial cosmic energy located in the individual.
- **KUTIR**: A small cottage; hut.
- **LAYA**: Merging; dissolution.
- **LINGA-SARIRA**: The subtle body, the astral body.
- **LOBHA**: Greed.
- **MAHA**: Great.
- **MAHABHARATA**: A Hindu epic.
- **MAHATMA**: Great soul.
- **MAITRI**: Friendship.
- **MANAS**: Mind.
- **MANONASA**: Destruction of mind.

- **MANTRA**: Sacred syllable or word, or set of words through the repetition and reflection of which one attains perfection.
- **MAYA**: The illusive power of God.
- **MOHA**: Infatuation.
- **MOKSHA**: Liberation.
- **MOUNA**: Vow of silence.
- **MOUNI**: One who observes silence.
- **MUKTI**: Liberation.
- **MUMUKSHU**: One who aspires after moksha or liberation.
- **MUNI**: An ascetic.
- **MURTI**: Idol.
- **NADA**: Mystic sound.
- **NIRODHA**: Control or restraint.
- **NIRVANA**: Liberation; final emancipation.
- **NIRVIKALPA-SAMADHI**: Super conscious state where there is no modification of the mind or Triputi.
- **NITYA-SIDDHA**: A liberated soul of marvelous powers who is ever present on the astral plane.
- **NIVRITTI**: Renunciation.
- **NIYAMA**: The second step in Raja Yoga; observance - purity, contentment, austerities, etc.
- **OM**: The sacred monosyllable which symbolizes Brahman.
- **PARIVRAJAKA**: Wandering monk.
- **PARAM-DHAMA**: Supreme abode.
- **PARAMAHAMSA**: The highest class of Sannyasins.
- **PASU-SVABHAVA**: Animal nature; bestial nature.
- **PATANJALI**: The author of Yoga-Sutras.
- **PRAKRITI**: Mother Nature, causal matter.

- **PRANA**: Vital energy; life-breath.
- **PRANAVA**: The sacred monosyllable Om.
- **PRANAYAMA**: Practice of breath-control.
- **PRATYAHARA**: Abstraction of senses; fifth step in Raja Yoga.
- **PREMA**: Divine Love.
- **PRITHVI**: Earth.
- **PURNA-YOGI**: A full-blown yogi.
- **PURUSHA**: The Supreme Being.
- **RAGA**: Attachment.
- **RAJA**: King.
- **RAJAS**: One of the three qualities of Prakriti which generates passion and restlessness.
- **RAJA-YOGA**: A system of Yoga generally taken to be the one propounded by Patanjali Maharishi, i.e., Ashtanga Yoga.
- **RAJASUYA-YAJNA**: A sacrifice performed by a monarch as a mark of his subduing all other kings.
- **RAMAYANA**: A holy narrative of Lord Rama.
- **RASA**: Taste.
- **RUPA**: Form.
- **SADHAKA**: Spiritual aspirant.
- **SADHANA**: Spiritual practice.
- **SADHU**: Pious man; Sannyasin.
- **SAGARA**: Ocean.
- **SAHASRANAMA**: The thousand Names of the Lord.
- **SAKTI-SANCHAR**: Transference of power by a developed Yogi.
- **SAMA**: Serenity; control of mind.
- **SAMADHI**: The state of superconsciousness where Absoluteness is experienced attended with all-knowledge and joy. Oneness.

- **SAMSARA**: The process of worldly life.
- **SAMSKARAS**: Impressions in the subconscious mind.
- **SAMYAMA**: Perfect restraint, an all-complete condition of balance and repose, concentration, meditation, and Samadhi.
- **SANKARA**: The well-known teacher of Vedanta philosophy.
- **SANKIRTAN**: Singing of divine songs.
- **SANNYASINS**: Those who have embraced the life of complete renunciation.
- **SATCHIDANANDA**: Existence absolute (Sat), Knowledge absolute (Chid), Bliss absolute (Ananda).
- **SATSANG**: Association with the wise.
- **SATTVA**: Purity - one of the three qualities of nature.
- **SATYA-YUGA**: The Age of Truth, the first of the four Hindu time-cycles.
- **SHABDA**: Sound.
- **SIDDHI**: Psychic power.
- **SIVA**: Lord Siva - bestower of auspiciousness on His devotees.
- **STOTRA**: Hymn.
- **SUDDHA**: Pure.
- **SUKHA**: Happiness.
- **SUTRA**: Aphorism.
- **SVADHYAYA**: Study of scriptures.
- **SVARUPA**: Essential nature; Reality.
- **TAMAS**: One of the three qualities of nature which generates inertia, laziness, dullness, and infatuation.
- **TANMATRA**: Subtle, undifferentiated root elements of matter.
- **TAPAS**: Austerity.
- **TAPASCHARYA**: Practice of austerity.

- **TATTVA**: Essence; principle.
- **TEHSILDAR**: Revenue officer.
- **TRIPUTI**: The triad - seer, sight, and seen.
- **TRISHNA**: Sense-hankering.
- **TURIYA**: The state of super consciousness, the fourth state transcending the waking, dreaming, and deep sleep states.
- **TYAGA**: Renunciation (of egoism, desires, and the world).
- **UDDALAKA**: A great sage of yore.
- **UPADESA**: Spiritual advice.
- **UPANISHADS**: Revelation; text dealing with Ultimate Truth and Its Realization.
- **VAIRAGYA**: Dispassion.
- **VEDANTA**: The school of Hindu thoughts (based primarily on the Upanishads).
- **VEDANTIN**: One who follows the path of Vedanta.
- **VEDAS**: The most ancient authentic scripture of the Hindus, a revealed scripture and therefore free from imperfections.
- **VEERYA**: Seminal energy.
- **YAMA**: First step in Raja Yoga; Eternal vows - non-violence, truthfulness, etc.
- **YOGA**: Union; union with the Supreme Being - any course that makes for such union.
- **YOGI(N)**: One who practices Yoga; one who is established in Yoga.
- **YONI**: Source.

References

1. Sivananda, S. (1992). The Principal Upanishads. The Divine Life Society.

2. Easwaran, E. (1987). The Upanishads. Nilgiri Press.

3. Mascaró, J. (1965). The Upanishads. Penguin Classics.

4. Hume, R. E. (1921). The Thirteen Principal Upanishads. Oxford University Press.

5. Radhakrishnan, S. (1992). The Upanishads, Volume 1. HarperCollins.

6. Gambhirananda, S. (1986). Eight Upanishads, with the Commentary of Shankaracharya. Advaita Ashrama.

7. Vivekananda, S. (1987). Vedanta: Voice of Freedom. Advaita Ashrama.

8. Easwaran, E. (2009). The Essence of the Upanishads: A Key to Indian Spirituality. Nilgiri Press.

9. Deussen, P. (2017). The Philosophy of the Upanishads. Dover Publications.

10. Prabhavananda, S., & Isherwood, C. (1947). Shankara's Crest-Jewel of Discrimination. Vedanta Press.

11. Sivananda, S. (2014). Upanishads: Gateway to Eternal Wisdom. The Divine Life Society.

12. Radhakrishnan, S., & Moore, C. A. (Eds.). (1957). A Sourcebook in Indian Philosophy. Princeton University Press.

13. Pai, R. (2019). The Vedas and Upanishads for Children. Hachette India.

14. Klostermaier, K. K. (2008). Hinduism: A Beginner's Guide. Oneworld Publications.

15. Panikkar, R. (1994). The Vedic Experience: Mantramañjari. Motilal Banarsidass.

16. Dasgupta, S. (1922-1955). A History of Indian Philosophy. Motilal Banarsidass.

17. Tolle, E. (1999). The Power of Now: A Guide to Spiritual Enlightenment. New World Library.

18. Desai, M. (2009). The Bhagavad Gita According to Gandhi. North Atlantic Books.

19. Prabhavananda, S., & Manchester, F. (1948). The Upanishads: Breath of the Eternal. Vedanta Press.

20. Vivekananda, S. (1989). The Complete Works of Swami Vivekananda. Advaita Ashrama.

21. Hodgkinson, B. (2006). The Essence of Vedanta. Arcturus Publishing.

22. Deutsch, E. (1980). Advaita Vedanta: A Philosophical Reconstruction. University of Hawaii Press.

23. Sarma, D. (Ed.). (2011). Classical Indian Philosophy: A Reader. Columbia University Press.

24. Sharma, C. (2000). The Advaita Tradition in Indian Philosophy. Motilal Banarsidass.

25. Pappu, S. S. R. (1962). Self-Knowledge in the Upanishads. Philosophical Library.

26. Murty, K. S. (1959). The Concept of Self in the Upanishads. Motilal Banarsidass.

27. Tharoor, S. (2019). The Hindu Way: An Introduction to Hinduism. Aleph Book Company.

28. Basham, A. L. (1954). The Wonder That Was India. Rupa Publications.

29. Radhakrishnan, S. (1995). Indian Philosophy: Volume I. Oxford University Press.

30. Prabhavananda, S. (1963). The Spiritual Heritage of India. Vedanta Press.

31. Eck, D. L. (2012). India: A Sacred Geography. Harmony.